惠赠：孙正earr和秦晖夫妇

"愿主耶稣基督的恩惠，

神的慈爱，

圣灵的感动，

常与你们众人同在。"

爱里有神迹！

6月6号18年

in Vancouver. CA

RESURRECTED

THE JOURNEY OF MIRACLES

Based on a true story

PETER PAN SHI

WESTBOW
PRESS®
A DIVISION OF THOMAS NELSON
& ZONDERVAN

WestBow Press books may be ordered through booksellers or by contacting:

WestBow Press
A Division of Thomas Nelson & Zondervan
1663 Liberty Drive
Bloomington, IN 47403
www.westbowpress.com
1 (866) 928-1240

ISBN: 978-1-9736-0456-3 (sc)
ISBN: 978-1-9736-0457-0 (hc)
ISBN: 978-1-9736-0455-6 (e)

Library of Congress Control Number: 2017915727

Print information available on the last page.

WestBow Press rev. date: 1/15/2018

My Wholehearted Thanks To

The Resurrected King Jesus Christ for the salvation of my life, God the Father, God the Son, and God the Holy Spirit.

The *sacrifice, patience, and unconditional love* from my special, beautiful wife Grace Pan Shi: a perfect helper assigned to me by God to walk with me through "good times and bad";

My beloved sons Simon and John Pan Shi for their great love;

Rev. Lee Stoneking, God's Apostle and Pastor Art Wilson, United Nations Miracle-Rev. for their Prophecies as light and courage for me to make this book a reality;

Senior Pastor Mark Ku and Pastor Zechariah Ku for their great teaching on God's Truth from Christian Zion Church Los Angeles, USA;

Paul and Janet Craig for their loving hearts and special efforts in proofreading and editing;

Apostle Roy Ying, Pastor Yizhen, Chen, Pastor Hsiu Hui Wu, Pastor Da Hai Zhou, Wang Zheng, Deacons Howard Wang and Michelle Lee, Dr. Zhou, Weiwu and Dr. Xue, Yanqun, Prof. Jerry Li, Herman and Lili Yang, Helen and Frank Hong, Reverend Michael T. Yu, Jin, Simon Lu, Mr. Sun, Zhengyan and Li, Hui for their great brotherhood and loving encouragement;

Many Dear brothers and sisters in different churches throughout the world, for their prayers in the Holy Spirit;

My parents, sisters and all my relatives and friends for their kind support;

Psalm 119:105

"Your word is a lamp for my feet, a light on my path"

****

Luke 24:6

"He (Jesus) is not here: *He has risen*"

Revelation 12:11

"They triumphed over him by the blood of the
Lamb and by the word of their testimony;…"

Hebrew 12:1

"Therefore, since we are surrounded by such a great cloud
of witnesses, let us throw off everything that hinders
and the sin that so easily entangles. And let us run
with perseverance the race marked out for us,…"

Luke 2:14

***"Glory to God in the highest heaven, and on earth
peace to those on whom his favor rests."***

PREFACE

My testimony is for those who are trying to find the one true God. May this be a great blessing to you and help bring you transformational life and growth, in accordance with His perfect will. My testimony is also written for my brothers and sisters in Christ, the devoted followers of Jesus Christ who are living in the Spirit of our Lord Jesus and in the Love of God.

This is a story that has been stored in my heart for more than twenty years. I have been waiting to tell this story, and through His grace, today, I joyfully share it with all of you. Whether you know it or not, you are deeply loved by the Almighty God, and He pursues each of you personally.

My heart has been urging me to release this story like "a fire in my bones" as a weapon helping us to stand firm to "extinguish all the flaming arrows of the evil one," "But if I say, 'I will not mention his word or speak anymore in his name,' his word is in my heart like a fire, a fire shut up in my bones. I am weary of holding it in; indeed, I cannot" (Jeremiah 20:9).

In the same way, the Apostle Paul says "For when I preach the gospel, I cannot boast, since I am compelled to preach. Woe to me if I do not preach the gospel! If I preach voluntarily, I have a reward; if not voluntarily, I am simply discharging the trust committed to me" (1 Corinthians 9:16-17).

There is an urgency within me to share how God saved me thirty-five years ago after suddenly collapsing; to awaken after thirteen hours of being in a severe coma, when the doctors didn't expect recovery at all.

From the moment of being released from the "Sting of death" up until now, I have been granted countless life miracles. All the glory belongs to our Lord. "My grace is sufficient for you, for my power is made perfect in weakness" (2 Corinthians 12:9). His grace is also available to you my dear brothers and sisters "For God so loved the world, that he gave his only Son, that whoever believes in him shall not perish but have eternal life" (John 3:16).

And now I am being prompted by The Holy Spirit, who spoke to me and commanded: "Now is the time to share your story of my power to resurrect you from thirteen hours of physical trauma and unconsciousness, and spiritual death to life. Now is the time to share your story of how I commissioned you to be a witness for me and give your testimony to all nations, that they might benefit from the revelation of my resurrection power." I am humbled at His mercy in revealing Himself to me and my heart answers loudly, "Yes I will! I am a "joyful slave and disciple to my MASTER…" I will obey Your commission to me." This then, is my story.

CHAPTER 1

"**Through** him all things were made; without him nothing was made that has been made" (John 1:3).

I WAS BORN IN A very poor, small, remote village in the south-eastern part of the People's Republic of China more than fifty years ago. I cannot remember many things that happened to me during that time, but I clearly remember my mother telling me that shortly after I was delivered from my mother's womb, my mother discovered an unexpected strange "water ball" on the top of my head. She was very afraid for me because in one week's time, this tumor on my head became bigger and bigger, and grew to the size of a "golf ball". The growth was a water ball tumor. My parents were very worried and concerned about this threat to my life. I was their treasured son, and they had big hopes and dreams for me. They couldn't understand why their beautiful and precious boy was subject to this abnormal growth and misfortune. My mother tried to be strong on the outside, but she would fall into a heap and sob deeply in private. At that time, my father who was dispatched for army duty, many miles away in a remote area, was despaired in hearing such bad news about his new born baby. He hadn't even met me in person yet.

My parents were completely unprepared as I was taken to the hospital and they struggled to watch me go through the operation to have the "water ball tumor" surgically removed from my head and the intensive care that followed. Perhaps they looked to a higher power for help. In the midst of their helplessness and devastation, perhaps they cried out for "Lao Tian Ye" (The Name of Father God in Chinese) or to whoever would help them, to save their precious child. "My life draws near to death; and You have put me in the lowest pit, in the darkest depths" (Psalm 88:3,6). God certainly must have been present to hear every cry and whisper for help. I was miraculously given my life back by God. The operation was successful, and God allowed me to survive without any side effects.

The Lord showed great mercy and compassion to me and my family. He saved my life on this earth because of his divine purpose for me, "For I know the plans I have for you," declares the LORD, "plans to prosper you and not harm you, plans to give you hope and a future. Then you will call on me and come and pray to me, and I will listen to you. You will seek me and find me when you seek me with all your heart. I will be found by you" declares the LORD, "and will bring you back from captivity..." (Jeremiah 29:11-14).

I was given back to my mother and she had the joy of seeing me heal and grow stronger. My parents were thankful to have me back, and as they treasured their son, there began to stir a reverence and awe of Father God. Little did they know there were still more trying circumstances to come.

CHAPTER 2

I WAS ABOUT FOUR YEARS old with little knowledge, let alone intentions, about life and the world, other than to help my mother. I was only a young shepherd in an isolated village, and I helped my mother tend to the two sheep we owned. I didn't know the meaning of life, what to eat, what to wear, nor did I have any thoughts about my future. I only thought about ways I could possibly help my mother and family. My mother is the kind of mother who showed her love to me and to her family by laboring and toiling in different farming jobs all day. She never once showed that she had any worries about our family's life or future, despite that fact that we lived in such a remote and poverty-stricken place. She has always had such a tender, merciful heart for everyone she meets, even up to the present day. "Blessed are the merciful, for they will be shown mercy" (Matthew 5:7). I have never heard any grumbling or complaints come from her mouth about anything. She has always been joyful, hopeful, and helpful to others when she is able. In her heart she fears "Lao Tian Ye".

She is a humble and delicate flower to my father, who is a strict disciplinarian. He disciplined me all the time and even does so to this day. He is a father full of love and compassion on the inside, yet always very stoic on the outside. My father is both a kind and strict father to me. His mission was to do his utmost to protect us and to provide a better life for his family.

My mother always looks beautiful to my father. My mother has a soft and gentle heart and spirit. She was a good and godly appointed match for my father, who was training in the Chinese army. He was rough around the edges and needed my mother's touch to keep him calm under pressure.

My parents had a small family wedding in town. They were married on a hill close by, where they would often dream about their future together. As a new bride, my mom wore a traditional Chinese gown with a red scarf that covered her whole head. My father proudly wore his uniform for the wedding ceremony. He looks so handsome in his wedding photos as a young officer and new bridegroom. They look so beautiful as a newly married couple. They were destined for a beautiful life ahead and had great things in store for them. They especially had high hopes for their children to come. For their first son, they dreamed he would be a scholar, or a professional of some sort. They knew all their children would be someone great, maybe even heroic. They loved to dream about their future and their future family. The Lord must have given them these dreams and desires. Certainly, the Lord showed his sovereignty and power as he listened to their conversations on the hill and as my life unfolded. He really loves my parents, and he loves me with an everlasting love.

When my father was dispatched to be on army duty, he was given very little notice. He left all the household responsibilities to my mother. My mother had to take care of my sister, my brother, myself and all the affairs of the household all by herself. It was a difficult childhood, but all my basic needs were met. My mom had such strength and stamina. She worked day and night to provide for our family, while my father was far away on duty. She would take the sheep out to graze and then bring them back for water. They needed the lush green grass so the milk would come. Sometimes I would go with her or do it myself. We searched for the greenest fields in the open wilderness. The sheep were our friends, not just our bread and butter. There were many times that we struggled. Being a farmer was hard because you were in it alone, for the most part. It was just you and your sheep. We didn't have a network of people supporting our business. My mother didn't have the encouragement or support she needed to keep plugging away. She had to find her strength somewhere else, or maybe in someone else. Perhaps she turned to the Lord for strength and perseverance. In any case, I am amazed at how hard my mom would work, day in and day out, to feed us and give us clean, simple clothes and clean water to drink. We always had food to eat from the previous year, until the famine. Before the famine, we had the best vegetables and lots of dates from the trees planted in our yard.

I didn't care much for weeding, but my mother looked so exhausted from being bent over in the hot sun for so long, that I would help her pull the never-ending weeds. Fresh vegetables were the best. It was worth the work. I especially enjoyed the taste of the vegetables in her spicy noodle soup and the juicy dates I would snack on throughout the day.

Some days as we were taking the sheep out, she would tell me how proud she was of me. She would share all the dreams she and my father had for me. They wanted the best life for my sister, my brother and me. They didn't want me to shepherd sheep for the rest of my life, spending my life here without many blessings from "Lao Tian Ye". I was not yet old enough to attend school with my brother and sister. So, in the meantime, I would follow my mother around, wherever she went, all the time.

The people in town and in the cities tended to look down on us. Somehow, they thought they were better than us, maybe because we lived on a farm and maybe because they knew my mother was on her own, taking care of all three children in my father's absence. My parents must have thought the same way, as they desperately wanted me to get a good education and leave one day. I didn't know any better at the time. To me, I was exactly where I wanted to be, with my mother, feasting on tasty dates and herding smelly sheep.

My mother never went to school. She longed to when she was younger, however, only boys were allowed to go to school when my mother grew up. She had big plans and dreams for me though. She really loved me. When we ate together, she would always give me the best part of the fruit. She would always take what was left over. She made sure I was fully satisfied before she would take the first bite of her meal. Her eyes danced with delight any time I spoke. She waited with baited breath to hear what I had to say. I was her miracle baby. I loved the smell of her hair and the touch of her natural curls that brushed my cheek when I would give her a hug. Even if we just came in from tending sheep or working the crops, I loved her familiar smell of grass, garden vegetables and fresh air. "I love you my sunshine" she would coo. "You bring joy and hope to my heart". "You are the man of the house when your father is away", she would say, "like a small angel comforting me." I wanted to please her. I wanted to make my mother proud. I wanted to fulfill her dreams for me.

One hot summer evening my mother and I were lying on our backs in our yard and saw two fighter jet planes shooting across the sky for some military training purpose. I asked my mom "how can I be like a bird, free to fly in the sky?" I thought to myself, when and how could I ever leave here for a new, better, and more beautiful place? I wanted to be like a bird flying in the sky, never worrying about anything. I dared to dream about one day being able to escape to a better place, far, far away. Now I know that "Although the Lord gives you the bread of adversity and the water of affliction, your teachers will be hidden no more; with your own eyes you will see them" (Isaiah 30:20). Our God promises in His word that "He will take pity on the weak and the needy and save the needy from death" (Psalm 72:13).

Like David was in the desert, I was a lonely shepherd in a small remote village in the wilderness, during the most difficult time of "China's Year of Famine" in the 1960s. I was sometimes cold, and sometimes had to bear the heat, but never with fear in my heart, or worry about tomorrow. I felt the support of my family's love (from our Lord Jesus who is always there shepherding us all the time to overcome and survive.) Even if you are suffering and toiling, He is still there for you as long as you approach Him and come before Him seeking His mercy, grace and help with a humble heart. "Rejoice in the Lord always. I will say it again: Rejoice! Let your gentleness be evident to all. The Lord is near. Do not be anxious about anything, but in every situation, by prayer and petition, with thanksgiving, present your requests to God. And the peace of God, which transcends all understanding, will guard your hearts and your minds in Christ Jesus" (Philippians 4:4-6).

I don't think that in those days my father and mother knew about

Christ, but they both feared "Lao Tian Ye" (Father God in heaven) in their hearts and obeyed all the rules and laws faithfully. They honored Him in their responsibilities to take care of their children with all their love and did so in God's righteous ways. "Listen to your father, who gave you life, and do not despise your mother when she is old. Buy the truth and do not sell it; wisdom, instruction, and insight as well. The father of a righteous child has great joy; a man who fathers a wise son rejoices in him. May your father and mother rejoice; may she who gave you birth be joyful!" (Proverbs 23:22-25).

The apostle Paul taught us in the Book of Ephesians: "Children, obey your parents in the Lord, for this is right. "Honor your father and mother" -- which is the first commandment with a promise -- "so that it may go well with you and that you may enjoy long life on the earth" (Ephesians 6:1-3). How important it is for a child to respect and honor his or her parents in Christ as God's child. The wisest man on earth, King Solomon, teaches: "My son, keep your father's commands and do not forsake your mother's teaching. Bind them always on your heart; fasten them around your neck. When you walk, they will guide you; when you sleep, they will watch over you; when you awake, they will speak to you. For this command is a lamp, this teaching is a light..." (Proverbs 6:20-24).

It was an idyllic childhood and I was soon to find out that God had bigger plans for my life.

CHAPTER 3

A S A YOUNG BOY, I loved to roam the countryside with my friends day and night. Once when I was six years old, I was walking with them through a cemetary, when suddenly a flash, "a ray of lightning" fell from the sky, right before my eyes. The strong light terrified me. I felt peace and calm on the inside, even though I was shaking on the outside. This was the first time I had ever seen such a flash of light. "Did you see that?" I asked my friends. "See what?" they asked me. "The big bright flash of light just now". "What are you talking about?" they jeered. "Let's get out of here, before you start seeing ghosts". I asked myself why no one else saw this vision but me? But I think this vision was a special gift that God gave to me, to see with my inner spiritual eyes. From that moment on I felt different. This was the beginning of a change that was happening to me on the inside. This was a very important gift given to me by the Holy Spirit.

For the first time in my life, I felt the desire to show mercy, love and kindness to others, as my mom had always shown to me and everyone around her. So, from then on, I sought to do good things for the people around me.

Looking back on this time, it reminds me of the passage of scripture when Jesus said to the seventy-two after they returned to him: "He replied, "I saw Satan fall like lightning from heaven. I have given you authority to trample on snakes and scorpions and to overcome all the power of the enemy; nothing will harm you"(Luke 10: 18-19).

What a wonderful promise and authority Jesus gave to those disciples. What a wonderful promise he gave to you and me. Have your spiritual eyes been opened? Are you spiritually alive in Christ? The apostle Paul prays in Ephesians that "I keep asking that the God of our Lord Jesus Christ, the glorious Father, may give you the Spirit of wisdom and revelation, so that you may know him better. I pray that the eyes of your heart may be enlightened in order that you may know the hope to which He has called you, the riches of his glorious inheritance in his holy people, and his incomparably great power for us who believe. That power is the same as the mighty strength he exerted when he raised Christ from the dead and seated him at his right hand in the heavenly realms..." (Ephesians 1:17-20).

Christ had begun to open my eyes and I was soon to put into practice this gift of generosity from God toward others, by helping a friend from the village.

CHAPTER 4

"A person's steps are directed by the LORD. How then can anyone understand their own way?" (Proverbs 20:24).

"Lord, I know that people's lives are not their own; it is not for them to direct their steps" (Jeremiah 10:23).

AS I MENTIONED, MY family lived in a very poor and small village. Sometimes my father would visit his close friend a few blocks away. I would often tag along to visit his son, Yang Guai, who became a close friend of mine.

Yang Guai was unable to walk because of an illness. He had to use wooden limbs to get around. It was difficult for me to comprehend why my neighbor was not able to move about freely with the same ease I was given. I felt sad for this boy who was confined to a chair, but I never looked down on him because he couldn't walk. My teacher taught me that "The attitude of your heart affects your mindset, and your mindset determines the decisions you make on how you treat others." I cherished and appreciated the fact that I could easily jump and run freely. I asked Yang Guai if I could help walk him to school. "Why would you want to do that?" he asked. "I don't know" I replied. "How else are you going to get to school?" So, every morning after breakfast, I would go to his house a few blocks away from mine and help him lean on my shoulders to walk him to school. Then I would bring him home after school every day. He leaned on my shoulders step by step for six years, every day to school and back. I did this without even thinking about it. I wasn't sure why I wanted to help Yang, or where my endurance and patience came from to do for six years straight. I didn't know why I felt compassion for Yang Guai. All I knew is I that wanted to help him. At the time, it was a real mystery to me, but looking back I believe the Lord must have given me a merciful heart and the desire and the strength help Yang. The Lord must have helped me to always "love my neighbor". I couldn't have done it of my own will or strength. Eventually we became very good friends.

Jesus taught us to "love Him and to love our neighbor as ourselves", and to even love our enemies! (Who today do you consider to be your neighbor? Is your "neighbor" your friend, colleague, peer, classmate, relative, spouse, child, acquaintance, stranger that crosses your path or even your enemy?)

As a teenager, my father decided I should get out of my comfort zone and move on and explore life outside of our tiny village. I was reluctant to leave the only home I had ever known, even though it was very poor and didn't seem like it had much to offer a young man. I had no choice but to follow my father's order to move to a big city called Shanghai in China. I felt very lonely, and was wondering how I could ever leave my village, and my friends.

Even though I didn't know God at that time, miraculously, God sent a very cute white dove to me one day. I was totally captivated by this dove. I couldn't believe my eyes as the dove flew and landed right beside me. I asked, "Lao Tian Ye" (Father God in Chinese), why this dove was in front of me? I felt a spark was ignited in my heart. Inside, I felt a burst of joy and excitement watching this dove. The bird was so beautiful with it's pure, white feathers. The dove somehow gave me a feeling of happiness and hope. This hope encouraged me to try my very best in my new life ahead. I felt the Lord had given me this dove as a gift, and I treasured it.

Also, in China there is a saying, "a dove can give you directions." As well, in the Bible, the dove can represent the Holy Spirit. The dove visited me many times, flying above and around my place. One day it was perched on the side of my door. I suddenly had the idea to tie something like a string to the dove's foot. It would be a personal sign for me to recognize my new best friend, should he return to me in the future. Without any resistance I was able to pick up the dove in my hand. It was so gentle and tame. I could not figure out why this beautiful bird was so calm in my hand and didn't try to fly away. After I tied the string to its foot, I lifted it up to the sky for it to fly away. Releasing the bird, I said, "Ok, my friend, if I am going to Shanghai, then you are going to Shanghai too." As it flew away I wondered if I would ever see my little friend again.

From that day right up until the day I was to leave for Shanghai I never saw the dove. My heart ached to say goodbye to my cute little friend. I was calm and cool on the outside, but inside I desperately wanted to see the dove one last time before my departure. On my last day at home, I deeply missed the dove, and regretted not having the chance to see it before I left. However, I paid a special visit to my other best friend Yang Guai to say, "so long". We hugged and although there was no exchange of words, tears streamed down our cheeks. Now that I was becoming a young man, my mom encouraged me not to cry, so I dashed to the car. We drove to the train station in silence. My whole family and I were going to take the train to Shanghai. I was sad but at the same time, I was also excited about the new life ahead of me.

The anticipation of a new adventure quickly faded however. In Shanghai, I had no friends. I was so very lonely. Here I was, completely alone, an introvert and afraid. I was used to my old school and helping my friend, Yang Guai every day to school and back. How I missed him. How I missed seeing that big smile on his face as I came through his door. How I missed the smell of sweet steamed buns, the mixture of smells of garlic, ginger, fried scallions, and steamed rice. I missed seeing his faded blue school bag and helping him onto his bench in his classroom. We had great conversations about what our moms made us for dinner and packed in our little light lunches. We would sometimes trade what we found in our lunches. I would give Yang Guai my egg pancake for steamed dumplings and rice noodles. If I was really lucky, I would trade my apple for a piece of fresh home-made bread.

We used to fly our kites together and when we played "going to town" a chase game, and "knocking the stick" with our school friends, I carried him on my back and ran as fast as I could. Yang Guai often had funny names for the stray dogs that would sometimes follow us to school. The roads were sometimes muddy, after a fresh rain and my shoes would sometimes get really dirty. But we didn't care too much about that. We loved to track our foot prints in the mud. During the cold and windy winters, we would make snow balls and see who could throw them the farthest. As the weather warmed up, we would sometimes search for wild blue berries on the way home. I can still taste the perfect mix of sweet and sour berries bursting with juice. I remember how refreshing the blueberries were after carrying Yang Guai on the dusty roads during the summer.

One day I was on the balcony of our new home in Shanghai, reminiscing about my childhood in the village, and surprisingly a dove landed right beside me. Feeling a little silly, I wondered, is this the same dove, my little friend? But how could it be possible for that dove to find me in this new place in Shanghai? How could the dove fly all the way from the village to this big city? How can a dove know me? As I carefully studied the bird, I couldn't believe my eyes… there, still wrapped around it's leg, was the string I had tied. My heart skipped! This made me wonder and ask, "could there really be a God that created the universe, who also knew me personally?" Did this God know what I was always thinking about? Did He know I was missing my friend Yang Guai so much? Did He know I was filled with sadness here in this new place? Did He know I was feeling desperately alone in the midst of the bustle and busyness of Shanghai? Did God know how I longed to be at my old home, in my old village with my friends? Did He send this beautiful dove to somehow let me know that not only does He know me and care about me, but this creator of the universe also pursues me? All I know is that I was changed from the first time I saw this "special dove". I was moved by the miracle of God sending my winged friend to encourage me. God gave me a very gentle and merciful heart. I learned from this experience, that whether you know or don't know God, He pursues you. He chooses you from the beginning, right from the time you are in your mother's womb.

Everything was new and interesting in Shanghai. I was very attracted to living in this big city nicknamed the "Pearl of the Orient". I wanted to find the most valuable pearls in this city, in the hopes of changing what I perceived to be a bleak future. Shanghai was so different from my village. It took some time to adjust to the massive population, modern buses, wide paved streets, tall buildings, and all the noise. I loved the smells that rose from the cake and the noodle shops. They were all new and exciting smells that awakened my nose. Being in the big city ignited all my dreams of making a name for myself. I strived to achieve success and to hopefully find more "pearls" in Shanghai, a place which was so beautiful and amazing to me. I felt like a "king" living in this great city, in a "palace" compared to the poor, small, remote, village I came from. I felt superior here and hoped to live the "Golden Life" in Shanghai. I felt excited about my new life, but little did I know, it was all about to change.

Chapter 5

AS MY FIRST YEAR at the new school came to a close, I wasn't too surprised that I didn't do very well. I think it is harder on students who transfer in from other regions of the country. I felt uncomfortable and very alone being a "foreign student" and unable to speak the local Shanghai dialect. It was easy for the locals to see I wasn't from there because of the language barrier. I'm not sure what they thought about me, nor did I care. I always just kept smiling and always hoped that I could someday build good friendships and fulfill my own dreams. Even if I wasn't as smart as they were, God must have given me wisdom. Somehow, I felt okay that my future and my way was different from theirs. "Yes, my soul, find rest in God; my hope comes from him" (Psalm 62:5).

One morning I woke up feeling quite good and in a cheerful mood. Summer had arrived and I was thankful for the break from homework, classes and feeling like an outsider. My heart was light, and optimistic. I woke up with more strength than usual. I felt a joy and focus as I showered and dressed to meet the day. I was a strong and healthy sixteen-year-old, excited to be here in Shanghai to seek my dreams of "digging out" more pearls for me and my family. This day had a special treat in store as I would be visiting one of Shanghai's neighboring cities and was about to set off on an adventure with my father's driver, Mr. Lin. We hopped in the car and the two of us drove off together. The sun was bright, and the cool breeze felt wonderful as we drove along. As we arrived, I felt elated to have the opportunity to visit this beautiful city I had never seen before. Our first stop was to a beautiful park with exquisite botanical gardens. We walked on the promenades bordering the water ponds filled with beautiful lily pads. We laughed as we noticed a family of three turtles sunbathing on a big rock that jutted out of the pond. We strolled into the pavilions and watched a young woman making pictures on thick parchment paper using ink. After about thirty minutes, we sipped on green tea and soaked in the lush smells of the plants and flowers we sat among. This was a relaxing and glorious escape from the big city that was now a part of my life. There were moments in the garden, I almost felt like I was back home in the village again. I was amazed to see the beautifully-designed gardens with a variety of flowers and trees, (looking back, I wonder if this was like the *"Garden of Eden"* in the Bible). I found my feet moving towards one of the traditional Chinese *"Temples"* that suddenly seemed to appear right in front of my eyes. I felt something strange happen as my eyes shifted away from admiring these beautiful natural gardens over to the gaudy, ostentatious construction that was encasing the "man-made idols".

I knew it was a temple, even though I had never been inside a temple before in my life. I didn't know God at this time but a temple in China is typically considered a "safe, lucky place." I was curiously drawn to go inside, and I went by myself to explore it, leaving Mr. Lin behind. The room was very dark, and filled with a strong-smelling incense and heavy silence. Instantly my body felt an icy chill. I had goosebumps on my arms. I felt my whole body start to shake the moment I took my first step into the temple. Feeling suffocated and taking very fast breaths, I was almost hyperventilating. I saw a line-up of many various idols against a wall. They were man-made statues that appeared to be made of copper. There was something like a hundred to a hundred and fifty of them. I turned around and scanned the room to see if there was anyone else in this big temple. There was no one there and even though it was 12:00 noon and it was bright and sunny outside, I felt a darkness closing around my heart. Surrounded by hundreds of these statues, which seemed to be intensely staring at me, I began to feel terrified, and my heart leapt, feeling like it might fly out my mouth. As I was standing there in disbelief, I had the eerie feeling that something bad was about to happen. The hairs on my neck were standing up, and alarm bells were going off inside me. The calm and joyful peace I woke up with this morning, had vanished. Dread flooded my body as I stood there wondering what on earth I was doing in this place. Suddenly, I was overcome with the desire to kick the idols. Even though I was very frightened, I used all the strength in my legs and feet to break them and knock them down. After I kicked the statues down, my whole body shook with terror. Gripped with fear, and shocked by the realization of what I had just done, I made a dash for it. I couldn't tell anyone. I felt so alone, even Mr. Lin didn't know what I had done. My heart was beating a like pounding drum. I escaped the building, but I kept the secret to myself. I returned to the car and thankfully Mr. Lin was still waiting for me. I jumped into the vehicle and pretended like nothing happened despite the perspiration on my forehead and my shaky hands. Mr. Lin didn't seem to notice. He looked like he had just woken up from a nap.

After leaving the temple, Mr. Lin took me to a quaint book store. I purchased a book about the city and then we made our way back to Shanghai. I started to read the book when I got home. Everything seemed normal. Around 7:30 pm that evening my parents were in the living room, and I was alone reading in my bedroom. I love to read, and I especially liked to read after dinner. I was deep into the book, when suddenly everything went black. I fell off my chair and crashed to the cement floor. For the next thirteen hours, I have no recollection of what happened. My father heard the loud noise of the impact of my body hitting the floor of my room and ran to see what was wrong. My parents were shocked to see me lying there motionless. My mother gasped in fear and worry at the sight of me and they rushed me to the hospital. Completely unconscious, I had no sense of being alive during those thirteen hours.

Chapter 6

WHEN I FINALLY OPENED my eyes for the first time after being unconscious, I could see a shining white light. In the brightness of this white light, I was stunned to see so many people around me. I saw my mom crying. I saw my family and friends all around me. They said they couldn't believe I was alive again. I didn't know what had happened or why I was in the hospital surrounded by all my family and friends. I could hear voices and hear my mom crying. "What's wrong? Where am I Mom?" I asked. "You collapsed" the doctor said, "but you are ok now". I realized at that point that I was in a hospital. "We thought we lost you" my mom cried softly. "You have been unconscious for thirteen hours". My mom's eyes were red and swollen, and she looked like she had aged a few years. She explained everything that had happened and how they carried me to the car to get to emergency. Strangely enough, from the moment I woke up out of the coma, I was filled with a joy in my heart and an energy that rushed through my body. My body felt so strong and alive. At the same time, I felt such peace. I felt completely transformed, resurrected, like I was given a brand-new life.

I didn't know it at the time, but as I look back, this awakening was the power of Jesus through the Holy Spirit giving me a miracle and bringing me back to life. I realized some time later, that life is Jesus and Jesus is our life. "because you will not abandon me to the realm of the dead, nor will you let your faithful one see decay. Therefore, my heart is glad and my tongue rejoices; my body also will rest secure" (Psalm 16:10, 16:9). Jesus said, "The thief comes only to steal and kill and destroy; I have come that they may have life, and have it to the full"

(John: 10:10). Praise the Lord that His grace and mercy brought back my life from this evil attack. "The salvation of the righteous comes from the LORD; he is their stronghold in times of trouble. The LORD helps them and delivers them; he delivers them from the wicked and saves them, because they take refuge in him" (Psalm 37:39-40). I was brought from death to life again to experience a new blessed life. God had a plan for my life.

After I came out of the coma, the doctors tried to figure out what happened to me. They did many tests to try to determine what caused a healthy and strong young man to fall into a coma without any warning or evident reason. The doctors did numerous examinations and tests on my body. They tried every possible means to determine what caused my 'sudden death'. The hospital that I was admitted to was the Huadong Hospital. This hospital was exclusively for the treatment of military soldiers and high ranked officers. This facility had the most advanced medical equipment, high-tech devices, and the most well-known specialists with the best expertise, ranking it one of the top hospitals in all of China at that time. Since I was part of a military family, I was privileged to receive treatment at this hospital.

Due to my unique case of "sudden death", the hospital formed a "Team of Specialists" to monitor, investigate and to examine my rare case of complete and instant recovery after thirteen hours of unconsciousness. They complied data daily through investigative means and advanced technological equipment to examine and test my brain, blood, intestines, bone marrow, etc. The doctors knew I was strong, young, healthy, and full of energy. I had no history of sickness or health challenges. I was confined to the hospital for about six months, and I was not allowed to leave. The team of specialists concluded after a period of half a year, that there was nothing wrong with my body or brain that could have caused this phenomena of "sudden trauma and death".

To this day it remains a "Mysterious Case". The chief doctor who treated me, Dr. Wu, (whom I went to meet in 2015 to verify this historical case), confirmed my story but unfortunately my "medical report" was lost. We had tried several ways to locate the "patient files" however over the thirty-five years of file relocation and reorganization we were unsuccessful in retrieving my file.

Dr. Wu emphasized that nobody on her team at that time, even up to now, ever met a special case like mine, and it is still a medical mystery. I brought back the photos I had of me and Dr. Wu. She described everything that happened in great detail. As I listened to her tell my story, I was again captured and in awe of God's mercy and love for me as he delivered me from the grip of death.

Even though the doctors, couldn't determine the cause of my sudden coma, we as followers of Christ, know that there is *Spiritual Warfare between the evil one and our Lord's Holy Spirit*. After a half year of confinement in the hospital, I was finally released to return to a normal life of high school studies without a medical diagnosis or explanation of my situation.

I believe it was a spiritual battle between the Holy Spirit and evil spirits. God used me and put me in this special position to reveal His glory. I was an innocent person and I kicked and broke many man-made gods in that temple. I believe the spirits of these idols were very angry with me and wanted to kill me. But God chose me, and He had His hand on my life. He saved me and brought me back to Himself. "He lifted me out of the slimy pit, out of the mud and mire; he set my feet on a rock and gave me a firm place to stand" (Psalm 40:2). "Blessed are those who have regard for the weak; the LORD delivers them in times of trouble. The LORD protects and preserves them – they are counted among the blessed in the land—he does not give them over to the desire of their foes" (Psalm 41:1-2). I can with every fiber of my being, assure you that my life and health was once again normal. I know from this experience that Jesus saved me and has victory over the forces of darkness, which we can't see with our physical eyes. There are great battles fought in the spiritual realms, but we don't need to fear or worry because Jesus chooses us and helps us overcome. Jesus will fight the spiritual battles for us. "The Lord will fight for you; you need only to be still" (Exodus 14:14). Jesus said

"And I tell you that you are Peter, and on this rock, I will build my church, and the gates of Hades will not overcome it. I will give you the keys of the kingdom of heaven; whatever you bind on earth will be bound in heaven, and whatever you loose on earth will be loosed in heaven" (Matthew 16:18-19). Hallelujah, what a great and powerful promise Jesus gives you and me for His purpose for us in this world.

After my stay at the hospital, I was thankful to find out that all the results were good and normal. I was so thankful to Jesus and know that it was Jesus who fought for me, saved my life, and gave me a second chance to live on this earth to testify to His power and love. I didn't know God at the time, but the Chinese talk about a "Father God in Heaven". Who is this Father? I don't know, but there is one in heaven watching over you, and taking care of you and protecting you day in and day out.

CHAPTER 7

I CONTINUED MY MIDDLE SCHOOL and high school studies and finished my education without any unusual incidents. However, I still was not able to adjust well from village life to city life. I was new to Shanghai and I felt out of place. I was like a fish out of water. I didn't make any friends and it was difficult for me to get to know my fellow students due to the language dialect barrier. I felt very isolated. Although I was in a school filled with so many students, my heart was very heavily burdened with loneliness. As I watched the students gather together in the lunch room, laughing and being silly, I longed to be a part of their conversations. I desired to belong to their groups. I buried my loneliness in the tantamount burden of studies in front of me. Despite feeling left out, I tried my best to study well, so I could get a good job in the future. I would make my parents proud of me yet. I would not disappoint them.

I spent two years preparing for college, but twice I was denied admission due to my low scores on the national admission's test. Going to college was my big dream and my parent's biggest hope for me, so I made up my mind to try one last time to prepare for the national examination with a shimmer of hope that I would be able to improve my scores enough to meet the admission requirements. When I got the results, I was again disappointed to find that my total score was still five points short of the score required for admission. I felt so frustrated and burdened and gave up all hope of attending college after receiving my results. Facing the fact that I would not be able to go college with the five-point difference, I started to give up on myself and I was reaching the lowest point of my life. It was this moment, that I felt deep down inside my heart, that I was the "biggest loser" on earth. "That is why, for Christ's sake, I delight in weaknesses, in insults, in hardships, in persecutions, in difficulties. For when I am weak, then I am strong" (2 Corinthians 12:10). God is so merciful and once again gave me hope. I was informed of a "special admission" from Shanghai Fudan University. It turns out that they reconsidered me as they granted ten points to my total scores based on my highest single subjective score on English. This was the best news I had ever heard! I was not prepared when the University officially informed me. It was like going from "impossible to possible" through the grace of our lovely Lord. Yes, "All things are possible with Him" and what our Lord of glory has prepared for us: "No eye has seen, no ear has heard, no mind has conceived what God has prepared for those who love him" (1 Corinthians 2:9). Our Lord can "change water to wine" instantly, according to His will. Our whole family was so excited and gave thanks to our Father in Heaven, calling me "a lucky dog"!

Unbelievably, I was accepted by Shanghai Fudan University to obtain an English Major. During my studies there, I expanded and developed a view and knowledge of a world outside of China. My mind was stretched to comprehend a larger scale of the world and I was about to see it with my own eyes.

CHAPTER 8

A S SOON AS I graduated from university, I was very blessed to obtain a job. I couldn't believe it. I was the only one chosen from the whole university to work for the local government in Shanghai. During that time in China it was such a privilege, honor, and good fortune to find a job working at a government office. I was given a position with the Shanghai Municipal Public Service. It was incredible to be given the opportunity as an ordinary university graduate, to work here. This position allowed me to meet with various heads of state. I met with presidents, ministers, ambassadors of China, all sorts of VIP high ranking officers visiting the Shanghai government. I was so proud of myself. I didn't know God. But as I look back, I ask myself why I was so blessed to get a job so quickly and felt that Jesus prepared this position for me. "He raises the poor from the dust and lifts the needy from the ash heap; he seats them with princes, with the princes of his people." (Psalm 113:7-8) I was such a young person but was being promoted so quickly and so often. I was promoted to a very high level early on in my career. Despite the overnight success, I always strove to do my best. I wanted to be the kind of person who would achieve everything strictly through my own abilities. I didn't want anyone else's help, because I didn't know God at that time.

After years of working for the Shanghai Municipal Public Service, I was given the chance to take some high-level exams to work at Commercial Services as a Foreign Consulate assigned and approved by the government of Shanghai as a local "international employee." This was a very, very competitive position. All the interested applicants were called together to take the examinations. There were four candidates, who I thought were all superior to me, in their experience and knowledge.

I was nervous about taking these kinds of exams. I knew I didn't study very well for them. But I challenged myself to take the exams anyway, and I was extremely blessed. It so happened that the very question on the exam paper was the exact same question I read and prepared for in my previous school years. Looking back, I know *the Lord was preparing me for something greater.* So, it was very easy for me to complete the examination. I was chosen to work as a commercial assistant at the Foreign Consulate, and the other four applicants were greatly disappointed. I don't think I was smarter or wiser, than the other applicants. I think God prepared me for this position. If you do your best, God will provide opportunities for you. "May your unfailing love be with us LORD, even as we put our hope in you" (Psalm 33:22).

I was working at a very high level for two different governments, as an international civil servant (called Local International Employees), for the U.S. and China. I was so young. I was the youngest staff member to serve in such a position in the whole city, even in the whole country at that time. I felt so blessed and privileged to have this amazing opportunity. I was not rich enough to buy a car on my meager salary in Shanghai, but the government provided me with my own car to "perform my duties". This was a gift and a dream come true. I was completely unprepared for the great blessings God gave me as my life transformed from one of poverty to one of luxury. I would often go to private official dinners in high class restaurants which were very expensive. I was vainly living a life of glory among all my friends and relatives. I felt like a kite flying so high, without boundaries. I was so proud of myself and my abilities. I thought it was my strength and intelligence that allowed me to make my own way, finding those valued and treasured "pearls" hidden in this big city. But now, as I look back, I see that it was all by God's grace and mercy that I achieved this position so early in my life and so quickly: We can only reach heights the Lord has prepared for us and strengthened us to fly to.

I don't know why God specially chose me from hundreds of thousands of people at that time, for this position. Maybe it was because my heart was full of love, gentleness, and mercy or more importantly, maybe it was because my heart fears "Lao Tian Ye" (Lord). I've come to know that He will keep me and protect me and that He has countless good things reserved for me. You can't do anything apart from God. When you love people, God will give you opportunities. "Every good and perfect gift is from above, coming down from the Father of the heavenly lights, who does not change like shifting shadows" (James 1:17). "Listen, my dear brothers and sisters: Has not God chosen those who are poor in the eyes of the world to be rich in faith and to inherit the kingdom he promised those who love him?" (James 2:5). Our Lord commanded "Love your neighbor as yourself" and that He would satisfy your desires by providing you the best opportunity for you in your life. As Ecclesiastes 12: 13 states "Now all has been heard; here is the conclusion of the matter: Fear God and keep his commandments, for this is the whole duty of all mankind." Daily prepare yourself to live in the love of our Lord, waiting for His best timing and the golden opportunities our Lord has specially prepared for you. "But from everlasting to everlasting, the LORD's love is with those who fear him, and his righteousness with their children's children-- with those who keep his covenant and remember to obey his precepts" (Psalm 103:17-18).

CHAPTER 9

I WAS FEELING VERY PROUD of myself, rubbing shoulders with so many high ranked government officials and diplomats. I had a position many people desired, and I felt inside my heart that I was better than everyone else. Proverbs 6:16-17 refers to six things the Lord hates, and one of them is haughty eyes. I didn't know I was being arrogant or disdainful at the time, but the Lord would soon show me the pride I carried in my heart.

Only God knows our steps. "In their hearts humans plan their course, but the Lord establishes their steps" (Proverbs 16:9). After about four years, there was a popular trend in Shanghai for young people to go abroad. I didn't like the idea of going abroad, especially on my own. I dreaded the thought of leaving this prestigious position in Shanghai with a great potential to be promoted to a state level high official of the Chinese government. I couldn't bear the thought of leaving my lovely family behind. I was torn because I was at a cross roads while at the highest peak of my career. But looking back on this, I see that God was calling me to leave China, that I may fulfill His purposes for me. However, it was still my decision to make. Should I leave everything I know and go to a foreign country, live among a different people with a different language and culture in the United States, to continue my studies and to broaden my views of the world? Should I give up all my vanity and my life of luxury here in Shanghai? Finally, after struggling day and night, with the choice I had to make, I decided to move to the United States, where there was "gold" everywhere so I was told. I thought having a high education and obtaining my Master's Degree in International Relations would also benefit me in the United States. This was the most "painful" and "glorious" decision I made in my whole life so far. This is a most difficult thing in life to do, to make a decision that may bring life or death to your future. Decision making should always be based on wisdom from the Lord. "The wisdom of the prudent is to give thought to their ways but the folly of fools is deception" (Proverbs 14:8).

Each of us has seven spiritual gifts from our lovely God, who is the greatest helper we could ask for. These gifts are there for you to call on whenever and wherever you need ---"the Spirit of the LORD, the Spirit of wisdom and of understanding, the Spirit of counsel and of might, the Spirit of knowledge and of fear of the LORD" (Isaiah 11:2). If you lack wisdom, then ask for wisdom, just like King Solomon did: "Give me wisdom and knowledge, that I may lead this people, for who is able to govern this great people of yours?" (2 Chronicles 1:10). Wisdom can be the key to the vital decisions you will make in your life. Where is the greatest wisdom? "The fear of the LORD is the beginning of wisdom, and knowledge of the Holy One is understanding" (Proverbs 9:10). Wisdom is now calling you and she is there for you, to help you make the right decisions on your way to success.

I came to the United States completely unprepared. My parents didn't want me to leave China by myself, without a marriage partner, so I quickly got married to a beautiful woman named Grace. We dated for one year in Shanghai, prior to my departure for the United States. This marriage was a great miracle and blessing to me back then and I am still now thanking God countless times for His amazing grace and mercy to me in my life for Grace. The Lord prepared me for my time ahead in a "foreign county" by placing Grace at my side to cling to in the tumultuous times that lay ahead of me. "Houses and wealth are inherited from parents, but a prudent wife is from the Lord" (Proverbs 19:14). We would be going to a "foreign land" without good friends or relatives to count on. My heart was troubled about this new "life adventure". I had mixed emotions about what lay ahead of us. I was confused, excited, and curious all at the same time. Random thoughts came to my mind: "Can I really find and dig gold? How much and when can I dig it out? Can I start a new life in this "land of freedom"? Can I survive there? Would anyone even notice if I died there?" The questions that ran through my mind were endless. I pondered them all as I traveled by plane over the Pacific Ocean enroute to the United States of America. Grace was not able to come with me right away, as securing her visa took a while. We didn't know it at the time, but it would be many months before she would get her visa and be able to join me in America.

Looking back, I know this call to leave China and go to the U.S. was from The Lord who called me at the right time to go to the right place. "There is a time for everything, and a season for every activity under heaven: a time to be born and a time to die, a time to weep and a time to laugh, a time to search and a time to give up, a time to tear and a time to mend, a time to love and a time to hate, a time for war and a time for peace" (Ecclesiastes 3:1-8). Yes, "Like a bird that strays from its nest is a man who strays from his home" (Proverbs 27:8). Like the story of God calling Abram to "Leave your country, your people and your father's household and go to the land I will show you. I will make you into a great nation and I will bless you; I will make your name great, and you will be a blessing. I will bless those who bless you, and whoever curses you I will curse; and all peoples on earth will be blessed through you" (Genesis 12:1-3). I am not at all as great as Abram, but God calls us all, as His children, in the same way to be used and to be set apart from this corrupted world. Finally, I obeyed and came to the U.S., where I had no idea if I could dig out a lot of gold, or whether or not I would even survive.

The U.S. is such a blessed and advanced country compared to China. The US. showed it's fear of the Lord when it established this great nation stamping "In God We Trust" on its citizen's hearts and on its national currency. "Blessed is the nation whose God is the Lord, the people He chose for His inheritance" (Psalm 33:12).

30 years ago, before I came to the U.S. I thought there would be "gold" everywhere in the United States. Not only was there no gold, but as soon as I took my first step on U.S soil at the San Francisco Airport I realized that I was all alone and my heart began to break. I suffered

unbearable loneliness in this foreign country without any friends or money at all. In China, I was proud and privileged to have a life of luxury, respected and honored by the people I met. I was treated like a king and was flying high in the sky. After only a short time living in the United States, I felt completely alone and miserable. It was such a culture shock when I moved from my life in Shanghai to my life in the States. It made me crazy. I wanted to leave. One day I couldn't stand the pain of being alone away from my wife, family, and my friends. I was so homesick that I called my father and told him "I want to come home Dad". I pleaded and secretly hoped he would fly me home instantly. However, my Dad said, "since you came all this way, you must stay and get your degree before you come back to China". I had very little money and couldn't afford to make that phone call. But what hurt even more, was the sting of his words which pierced my heart. After I hung up I wept until I fell asleep. This was the first time in my whole life I had ever felt this lonely. I was emotionally broken, weary, and almost penniless.

The first school I was accepted to was the University of Tennessee. I had no extra money to take a flight there, so I took a Greyhound Bus for four days to Tennessee from San Francisco. I spent most of what little money I had saved up, on the bus trip, the tuition, and the books. Since my finances were lacking, I couldn't take regular classes but rather enrolled in the intensive classes which were not as expensive. Even though I was many miles from the home that I knew and loved, God knew exactly where I was. One day as I was walking on the road with another student, we ran into someone named Matthew. He asked me if I was from China. I said "Yes, from Shanghai. Do you know where Shanghai is?" He surprised me by answering "No". This seemed like the strangest thing to me because I thought everyone knew where Shanghai was.

Matthew saw that we had nothing to eat and without another word he took us to the super market to buy us some food. He also gave us a ride back to our "trailer dorm." I wondered who this person and what motivated him to help us. But I accepted his charity because I was hungry most of the time, and desperately needed the food. I couldn't figure out why Matthew was being so kind to me. I didn't know him.

Back in China, I had never experienced this kind of generosity from a complete stranger, but despite my inability to understand this curious man, Matthew always came back to help us. I couldn't figure him out. I thought maybe there was something wrong with the guy. Later, I learned that he attended a local church. Matthew kept inviting me to come to his church, but I insisted that I didn't want to go. Unfortunately for me, I didn't accept his invitation to visit his church at that time, however, my other two roommates did go to church with him.

I had nothing healthy to eat in my trailer. For three months, I ate cabbage with ketchup between two pieces of bread for breakfast and lunch. It was Christmas Eve which seemed to be a big deal in the United States. The Americans decorated their houses on the outside with colorful, bright lights. They also decorated pine trees and plunked them in the middle of every store and building possible. Matthew never gave up on me and invited me to church for a Christmas Eve dinner. I was so hungry that I relented. After all, I thought, surely the meal at the church couldn't be worse than my cabbage and ketchup sandwiches. I was met with the most incredible smells, when I walked through the door. I was overwhelmed and ecstatic at all the delicious turkey, stuffing, and taste sensations as I experienced them for the first time. It didn't even matter to me that this meal didn't include rice, dumplings, or noodles. The large American portions made up for it. I was physically starving for food as well as hungering for love, purpose, and friendship. My first big feast was in church. At that time, I still didn't know God, but God had prepared that day for me to show me His love; that there is a place for me, a purpose, and a future for me. God sent Matthew to extend His love to me in my time of need. I will never forget God's kindness afforded to me when I was physically and emotionally empty, struggling and starving. However, I didn't go to church after that. I was transferred to a University in Boston. I continued my studies and worked part-time on campus at the same time. However, my adventure was about to continue in 'The Cradle of Liberty'.

CHAPTER 10

"Some wandered in desert wastelands, finding no way to a city where they could settle. They were hungry and thirsty, and their lives ebbed away" (Psalm 107:4-5). "And You put me in the lowest pit, in the darkest depths" (Psalm 88:6). "For my soul is full of trouble and my life draws near the grave" (Psalm 88:3). "From my youth I have been afflicted and close to death; I have suffered your terrors and am in despair" (Psalm 88:15).

"The Lord is gracious and righteous; our God is full of compassion. The Lord protects the simple hearted; when I was in great need, He saved me. For you, Lord, have delivered my soul from death, my eyes from tears, my feet from stumbling, that I may walk before the Lord in the Land of the living" (Psalm 116:5-8).

I WAS MISERABLE IN BOSTON and my heart grew faint in despair. Thankfully, eight months into arriving, Grace, my beautiful bride, received her visa and left China to support and help me. Having Grace with me made all the difference. Even though the Lord was always with me, protecting and caring for me, Grace was someone physically there to comfort me in my weakness and depression in this "Beantown" (Boston's nickname) "even though there are no 'Beans' for us to eat here" she joked. Her beautiful smile, kindness, deep love for me, and sense of humor, was such a ray of light during those dark days. I began to feel like a real man again. I stood and felt taller when she was beside me. I was proud to have her beside me wherever we went. She was a precious gift from the Lord, and I didn't know it back then, but God blessed me immensely with Grace. Hereby, I cordially use the Scripture quoted from "Song of Songs" as my great thanks to my beautiful wife Grace, and I hope each husband is also thankful for God's grace to have such a great and beautiful helper specially assigned to be united with them.

"You have stolen my heart, my sister, my bride, you have stolen my heart with one glance of your eyes, with one jewel of your necklace. How delightful is your love, my sister, my bride! How much more pleasing is your love than wine, and the fragrance of your perfume than any spice! Your lips drop sweetness as the honeycomb, my bride; milk and honey are under your tongue. The fragrance of your garments is like that of Lebanon. You are a garden locked up, my sister, my bride; you are a spring enclosed, a sealed fountain. Your plants are an orchard of pomegranates with choice fruits, with henna and nard, nard and saffron, calamus and cinnamon, with every kind of incense tree, with myrrh and aloes and all the finest spices. You are a garden fountain, a well of flowing water streaming down from Lebanon" (Song of Songs 4:9-15).

Grace is the most beautiful woman in the world to me and she strengthens me with her love. "Many waters cannot quench love; rivers cannot wash it away" (Song of Songs 8:7). The power of love is your strength, hope and a help in all times, in all situations. Love is a miracle and power that never fails you.

As a husband, I wanted Grace to be comfortable in Boston. It was tough for her also to adjust to a new country. She didn't have her friends or family to turn to either. When she arrived in Boston, she didn't speak very much English and found it hard to communicate with other people in everyday situations. However, she was strong and determined to make our lives workable and better in Boston day by day.

Grace has always been so calm, and elegant even when she is cooking and taking care of our home. I love to come home to the smell of her cooking. Somehow, when we are together, the worries and challenges melt away, even if only for a few hours.

Grace was also very patient with me. When I got frustrated with school, she was able to help me forget and move on. I am so thankful she was there with me. She encouraged me and made me want to be a better man; a man with hope. "I wanted to give Grace the best life", I thought to myself. I want to prove to her she made the right decision marrying me. I want to give and share everything with her. She is my princess, and I want to make all her dreams come true.

To help support my wife and I, I took a part-time job at a Chinese restaurant. I worked during the day and took classes in the evening. It was very laborious for me, a thin person about 110 lbs. I was hired as a delivery boy for a Chinese restaurant. One windy and snowy afternoon, as I was riding my bicycle to deliver food from the restaurant along on Beacon St., I thought about how in China I was treated like a king in the highest, but in Boston, I definitely felt more like a delivery boy. These thoughts made me crazy, but I didn't know how to deal with the bitterness I harbored in my heart. My motivation in taking this job, was based on the hunger pangs I felt when I went without. I had a goal to meet before I could return to China. My parents were expecting me to fulfill my dreams of "big success, fame and a glorious homecoming." I had no choice but to work to earn a living. It didn't help that I was also so home sick for my mom, dad, my brother, and my sister. I didn't expect to suffer so greatly here in Boston and I didn't see how it could get any worse.

As I was shivering and riding along in the winter storm, making a delivery of sweet and sour shrimp, egg foo young and chicken fried rice, I was hit by a yellow cab. I was thrown about fifty feet across the street. I was flying in the sky along with the take-out boxes once secured to my bike. I fell to the ground. As my whole body shook, a thought crossed my mind that made me smile on the inside, because I thought of the opportunity and possibility that this accident might bring with it. Perhaps I could sue this driver and my financial problems would be over. A man is born with greed from the moment he takes his first breath. Just like the Scripture said in Jeremiah 17:9 "The heart is deceitful above all things and beyond cure. Who can understand it?" But "I the Lord search the heart and examine the mind, to reward a man according to his conduct, according to what his deeds deserve" (Jeremiah 17:10).

I was rushed to the hospital for emergency treatment at the Intensive

Care Unit and was hospitalized for a few days without any broken bones. "The Lord is close to the brokenhearted and saves those who are crushed in spirit, A righteous man may have many troubles, but the Lord delivers him from them all; he protects all; he protects all his bones, not one of them will be broken" (Psalm 34:18-20). As it turned out, it was actually my fault that I was hit. I couldn't sue the driver after all and as I lay in my hospital bed, I fell deeper into depression.

After being released from the hospital, I realized I only broke my eye glasses, and my fingers were a bit hurt, but my life was saved. Perhaps there was still hope for me after all. I was overwhelmed with grace and the sense that God always protects. God gave me a miracle and saved my life according to his will again, with his amazing grace. "The Lord will keep you from all harm-He will watch over your life; the Lord will watch over your coming and going both now and forevermore. The Lord watches over you-the Lord is your shade at your right hand; the sun will not harm you by day nor the moon by night" (Psalm 121: 5-8).

CHAPTER 11

AFTER THE ACCIDENT, I felt this job was too dangerous for me, so I decided to quit and began to work part-time for a gemstone company as an indoor sales person during the day. I continued to pursue my Master's degree in the evenings. I worked hard during the day and studied hard in the evening. One night, about 11:00 pm when my class ended, I took the subway and needed to walk through an empty parking lot to my home. Leaving the subway, there was a young man with a slight build, named Tan, who was walking in the same direction I was. We walked together across a playground sharing a little bit about our backgrounds. I learned he was from Malaysia. We quickly connected as we compared our stories about the necessary adjustments we had to make to the new culture and cooler climate. As we reached the middle of the parking lot we met a group of men. The hair on my neck stood up. There were eleven or twelve young men circling us. My initial instincts told me that my life was going to end tonight. One larger and muscular man said, "give me all your money now or you're dead!" I panicked and asked Tan what we should do, knowing I had no money to give them. Tan reached into his jacket pocket and pulled out a small hand gun. The men seemed surprised and wasted no time running away. Tan quickly escorted me to my apartment.

My life was spared once again. When you think there is no hope and you can't do anything, God protects you and saves you. He is with me in the valley, so I don't need to worry about life-threatening situations and difficult circumstances. This was the most dangerous situation I encountered during my time in Boston. I may have been killed if it hadn't been for this young man from Malaysia. God had intervened to help me escape unscathed once more.

This was yet another miracle the Lord provided for me. "The Lord rescues the life of the needy from the hands of the wicked" (Jeremiah 20:13B) and he sends/ uses men like angels to protect our lives from trouble. "See, I (the Lord) am sending an angel ahead of you to guard you along the way and to bring you to the place I (the Lord) have prepared" (Exodus 23:20). "For I hear many whispering, 'Terror on every side' they conspire against me and plot to take my life. But I trust in you, Lord; I say, 'You are my God'" (Psalm 31:13-14).

It is very humbling to think that despite thousands of people dying every day, God would choose to send an angel to protect me. "Are not all angels ministering spirits sent to serve those who will inherit salvation?" (Hebrews 1:14). "If you make the Most High your dwelling -even the Lord, who is my refuge- then no harm will befall you, no disaster will come near your tent. For he will command his angels concerning you to guard you in all your ways; they will lift you up in their hands, so that you will not strike your foot against a stone. You will tread upon the lion and the cobra; you will trample the serpent. Because he loves me" says the Lord, "I will rescue him; I will protect him, for he acknowledges my name. He will call upon me, and I will answer him; I will be with him in trouble, I will deliver him and honor him with long life, I will satisfy him and show him my salvation" (Psalm 91:9-16).

While I was at Northeastern University in Boston, I had big dreams to work as an international civil servant in the international communities, where I thought love, peace and happiness existed. I pursued my dreams, and applied for an internship position at an international organization United We Stand (UWS). Due to my background, I was very fortunate to be accepted with sixty other interns from all over the world. I fulfilled my dreams of becoming a goodwill ambassador at UWS. In 1994, I had an eight-month internship there. It gave me a lot of confidence to pursue a new life. I was so proud of myself. I was very prideful and arrogant. I thought I could do everything and anything myself. I basked in my smugness and thought about how smart I was to obtain such a position at this prestigious organization in only two short years of being in the

U.S. After the internship program was over, I continued my studies until I was officially hired by the organization in 1996. But after a short time, I was let go, without any obvious reasons that I could discern. So just as quickly as I went up, I came crashing back down, feeling like my life was without any hope of a future.

At the time I didn't understand why God "kicked me out" of the organization while a few others continued to work as employees. It is true that sometimes there are things we can't figure out on our own... why? why? why? "The lot is cast into the lap, but its every decision is from the Lord" (Proverbs 16:33). "The king's heart is in the hand of the Lord; he directs it like a watercourse wherever he pleases" (Proverbs 21:1). We do not need to waste too much time asking "why? why? why?", but we must humble and submit ourselves under God's mighty hand, "that He may lift you up in due time. Cast all your anxiety on Him because He cares for you" (1 Peter 5:6-7).

My inability to remain at this amazing organization was like a kick to the stomach. I lost all hope and wanted to return home to China as my only way out. I was at my lowest point of despair. I was out of a job, and out of money. I couldn't get out of bed for almost a week. I just wanted to disappear. I had no hope and my dream and initial faith faded away in seconds. I was no longer that man with confidence. I was no longer proud or arrogant. I felt my future and my life ripped out from under me. "For my thoughts are not your thoughts, neither are your ways my ways," declares the Lord. As the heavens are higher than the earth, so are my ways higher than your ways and my thoughts higher than your thoughts" (Isaiah 55:8-9). "Before his downfall a man's heart is proud, but humility comes before honor" (Proverbs 18:12). and "Pride goes before destruction, a haughty spirit before a fall" (Proverbs 16:18).

I was becoming a shell of a man and I didn't feel like I had accomplished anything here in the United States, or had any hope of realizing my dreams. I just wanted to end my life here and go home with my wife to China.

Chapter 12

OUR GOD IS SO awesome! He knows us inside out. He knows
our very thoughts, the longings in our soul and every cell in our
body. He can sustain us during our weakest times and lowest points in
life. My adventurous life in Boston was nothing short of miserable, but
sometimes what seems like a complete mess to us is part of God's bigger
plan; one that will eventually save us and deliver us out of our troubles.
Sometimes I couldn't understand why God put me in such a painful
situation. Looking back, I realize that it was his perfect purpose and
plan of "humbling me and testing me, in order to know what was in
my heart, whether or not I would keep his commands" (Deuteronomy
8:2). "See, I have refined you, though not as silver; I have tested you in
the furnace of affliction" (Isaiah 48:10). He promised to sustain us and
will surely open a new door for us. "See, I am doing a new thing! Now
it springs up; do you not perceive it? I am making a way in the desert
and streams in the wasteland, to give drink to my people, my chosen,
the people I formed for myself that they may proclaim my praise"
(Isaiah 43:19).

It was during my most difficult time that I was fortunate to be able
to connect with a kind Jewish man; Mr. David J whom I just met once
in Shanghai. I randomly found his business card one day and asked
him if we could meet for coffee. It turns out he was very well off and
he extended much kindness and generosity to Grace and me. He invited
us out for some delicious dinners at some very high-class restaurants.
I asked him why he was treating Grace and I so lavishly. I couldn't
understand his extreme generosity towards us. David told me he was

touched by my merciful and gentle heart. I had helped David with travel arrangements and train schedules, when we first met in Shanghai 2 years ago. David had an interest in making good Asian friends, so he could learn more about the Asian culture.

Surprisingly, He offered me a large sum of money to finance my school tuition fees. I wasn't comfortable with accepting his offer. My pride and dignity wouldn't allow it. He told me that he felt called to help me financially. He had never met anyone like me and Grace before. Since I didn't feel comfortable accepting his money, he showed his kindness to us by inviting Grace and I to travel with him. He escorted us on extravagant, private trips. He showed us the beauty of this glorious land in the different States of America. He took care of our accommodations in five-star hotels. Once he even put us up in the presidential suite.

The Lord used David to give me hope to continue to live on. I was feeling very low during this time of my life, and the Lord brought him to me like a precious and merciful gift. Even though I was suffering, God surrounded me with someone who changed my life and gave me hope. We became very good friends. I had never met anyone like him before in all my life. Sometime after being saved, I shared Jesus with him and what Jesus had done for me in my life. However, I'm not sure if he ever opened his heart to the truth and light of Jesus.

The Lord was so gracious to me. At that time, although I couldn't give Grace an extravagant holiday like this on my meager income, God allowed me to treat Grace to gourmet feasts prepared by chefs, graciously extended to us by David. He allowed me to treat Grace to a two-week vacation, where she wouldn't have to make the bed, vacuum, dust, cook, or clean toilets. The Lord gave me my heart's desires of giving Grace the best life, even if it was only for two weeks. It came at a time when even I couldn't have planned it better in my wildest dreams. Is this awesome and amazing or what? God will put people in your path to bring you hope and give you a thankful heart.

As a Jewish man, David is very disciplined in obeying the Law of Moses. Although David is not a believer yet, he knows of our Lord Jesus and I pray for God's mercy and salvation for him. This is my biggest prayer for David. He knows this truth from the Law of Moses: "when an alien lives with you in your land, do not mistreat him. The alien living with you must be treated as one of your native-born. Love him as yourself, for you were aliens in Egypt. I am the Lord your God" (Leviticus 19:33).

Chapter 13

WHILE PURSUING MY STUDIES in Boston, on top of feeling depressed, my health was beginning to deteriorate. One night around midnight, I was awakened by an excruciating pain. It felt like my big toe was being stabbed with a pin. It was red and swollen, and I didn't know how to make the pain go away. I was so desperate that I called my neighbor for help. He came over immediately and drove me to emergency on his bike. The time in the waiting room seemed to go on forever. Finally, it was my turn. The doctor examined me and diagnosed me with GOUT – one of the most painful forms of arthritis. He gave me an injection, which brought me some relief. He also prescribed some medication for me to take and then sent me home.

Shortly after this happened, Grace and I, who had been discussing a move to Los Angeles decided to take the plunge. Our small family of three, made the trek across to the other side of America. After two months, the symptoms appeared again, but the pain in my big toe was even more severe. I realized it was the gout starting again, so I took the medication. For some reason, the meds made me nauseous and I couldn't keep anything down. My body rejected every prescription I tried so I decided to try a Chinese doctor. "Maybe he can heal me", I thought to myself. But the Chinese doctor couldn't help me either. I came home to our rented basement suite and went straight to bed. I laid down for a month and a half unable to move. This was the second time I cried. I thought my life would end, as the pain became more and more severe. I even considered cutting my toe off in my desperation to stop the pain.

"If I don't do something now, I will not make it", I thought, so I started packing my bags to go back to China. As I bent over and started to gather my clothes and books, a flyer fell out of my pocket. I had received this flyer six months ago at a Chinese Super Market. At that time, I didn't feel comfortable throwing away the flyer, so I kept it in my pocket. The flyer that fell out in front of me said that "Jesus can save you and heal you". Grace saw it and said, "Jesus can save us all, let's go to church". "That's a lie" I responded, groaning miserably, "No one in this world can save us or heal my pain."

On two different occasions, evangelists came to our place to share the gospel with us. I kicked them out, even though they didn't give me any reason to disrespect them. I believed in nothing but myself. I certainly didn't want to go to church, but my wife (my dearest, wise wife) did. She hid this part of her life from me. As the head of the household, I had warned her previously not to go to church. But "The wise woman builds her house, with her own hands the foolish one tears hers down" (Proverbs 14:1). I had no idea she had been praying for me for about two weeks. This was such a painful part of my life. I felt hopeless and couldn't see a way out. Through Grace's strong encouragement, and wanting my pain to end as soon as possible, I finally relented and went to church with her. "For there the Lord bestows his blessing, even life forevermore" (Psalm 133:3B). This was my first time to go to Christian Shiloh Church, a Chinese community church, in San Francisco.

CHAPTER 14

WHEN I APPROACHED THE church, I could hear everyone worshipping and praising someone. As I took my first steps into the church, I felt something touch my hand, head, and my whole body. Tears came flooding out. Suddenly, my whole body was shaking. I was so joyful, so peaceful and happy in my heart for the first time in my life. I had never experienced these feelings before. Suddenly, my mouth opened, and these strange murmuring sounds came out. They were random, nonsensical sounds. I started to "speak in tongues." I didn't even know what speaking in tongues was. I felt kind of strange speaking such strange sounds. I spoke in tongues for nearly three hours until I returned to our home. I lay on my bed unable to control myself. My whole body was still shaking, while I spoke in tongues without ceasing.

Both Grace and I felt very scared. We had never encountered such a strange phenomenon, so Grace called the church. She described what was happening to me, and asked them what was going on. She asked if somebody could help stop my crazy gibberish and stop my body from shaking. The person answered excitedly and with laughter in his voice, said: "this is normal, don't worry, your husband will be all right. God has chosen your husband and he can't escape." We felt kind of relieved by his words and gradually I returned to normal while lying in bed.

Strangely, I felt something (the painful evil spirit) come out of my big toe and I was starting to feel comfortable. My pain was subsiding, and I fell into a deep sleep. How mysterious it is "to speak in tongues"! It felt like I was uttering a foreign language. It is only now that I understand the powerful spiritual gift God gave me so graciously, when

I was first touched by the Holy Spirit. When you speak in tongues, that is your spiritual interaction with the Holy Spirit to: "edify yourself"; to "declare and praise the wonders of Almighty God;" to "speak to God not to men;" to "pray for other people who don't know the Holy Spirit;" to "utter the mysteries of the Lord's Kingdom" and to "drive out demons". If the Lord has bestowed this gift upon you, how great and wonderful is the Holy Spirit's manifestation of speaking in tongues.

I thank God that I frequently speak in tongues in private. But I do not speak it in the church, as the Apostle Paul teaches us not to. However, I find that praying in the Holy Spirit, as I speak in tongues nurtures my relationship in a deeper way with my Lord.

I was baptized by the Holy Spirit, but was totally unprepared for it. Sometime later, I was baptized in water. In exactly the same way, Saul was baptized by the Holy Spirit on his journey to Damascus: "As he neared Damascus on his journey, suddenly a light from heaven flashed around him. He fell to the ground and heard a voice say to him, 'Saul, Saul, why do you persecute me?'" (Acts 9:3-4). "Immediately, something like scales fell from Saul's eyes, and he could see again. He got up and was Baptized, and after taking some food, he regained his strength" (Acts 9:18).

By being baptized in the Holy Spirit and water, washing his sins away and calling on Jesus, Saul was transformed into a new person in Christ. Jesus gave him a new name. He changed his name from Saul to Paul. He was transformed from a persecutor of the church to a devoted follower of Jesus Christ. Jesus commissioned Saul to do something extremely important. The Lord told Ananias to instruct Saul "Go! This man is my chosen instrument to carry my name before the Gentiles and their kings and before the people of Israel. I will show him how much he must suffer for my name" (Acts 9:15-16). What a calling for Saul! It is true today that the Lord will also call you and me to "suffer for his name and kingdom" in this evil and twisted generation. Have you ever felt suffering and persecution for His kingdom? If so, you are positioned to receive and enjoy all the grace and blessings in His Kingdom. It is Paul's view that all glory and miracles come after suffering. "So, I find this law at work: when I want to do good, evil is right there with me.

For in my inner being I delight in God's law; but I see another law at work in the members of my body, waging war against the law of my mind and making me a prisoner of the law of sin at work within my members. What a wretched man I am! Who will rescue me from this body of death? Thanks be to God- through Jesus Christ our Lord!" (Romans 7:21-25).

Peter said: "Therefore, since Christ suffered in his body, arm yourselves also with the same attitude, because he who has suffered in his body is done with sin" (1 Peter 4:1). Suffering is worth it, because it helps us grow to be more like Jesus Christ.

The Lord's great commission to each of his followers is a great blessing and we must obey and act in His truth and Spirit. "Woe to me if I do not preach the gospel" as "The gospel is the power of God for the salvation of everyone who believes" (Romans 1:16). "Now to him who is able to establish you by my gospel and the proclamation of Jesus Christ, according to the revelation of mystery hidden for long ages past, but now revealed and made known through the prophetic writings by the command of the eternal God, so that all nations might believe and obey him - to the only wise God be glory forever through Jesus Christ! Amen" (Romans 16:25-27).

You may sometimes feel too weary, lack power, or feel that you are too busy (just excuses) to spread and share this gospel to your neighbors, but God will strengthen and restore you with his Holy Spirit: "But you will receive power when the Holy Spirit comes on you: and you will be my witnesses in Jerusalem, and in all Judea and Samaria, and to the ends of the earth" (Acts 1: 8). Our Lord promises everyone, including you and me as we seek His Holy Spirit, that He will build up our faith through his word "In the last days, God says, I will pour out my Spirit on All people" (Acts 2:17). By our actions, we shine like stars in this dark evil world. "So that you may become blameless and pure, children of God without fault in a crooked and depraved generation, in which you shine like stars in the universe as you hold out the word of life..." (Philippians 2:15). "Whatever happens, conduct yourselves in a manner worthy of the gospel of Christ. Then, whether I come and see you or only hear about you in my absence, I will know that you stand firm in the one Spirit, striving together as one for the faith of the gospel" (Philippians 1:12,27).

The baptism of this Holy Spirit totally transformed my life and made me a new person. I was not ready for this and knew nothing beforehand about what was happening to me or why. I didn't know why God loved me so much. He was cleansing me of all my sins on the inside. I confessed to God so many things that were hidden deep in my heart. I really wanted to become a new person and was thirsty for a new life. After going to church three or four times, my pain left without the use of medication. This encouraged me tremendously in my faith in God. Who is this healer? Who is this Jehovah Rapha? Who is this Jesus who can heal your body physically and spiritually? He healed me physically and I began to experience more of God in the Holy Spirit.

Grace, and I were water baptized together, one month after we began attending church. *Baptism is a most wonderful step and declaration of your commitment to Jesus.* We learned to pray and fellowship with our brothers and sisters in Christ. We attended a church Bible study and started sharing the good news of the gospel of Christ.

Chapter 15

"And do not grieve the Holy Spirit of God, with whom you were sealed for the day of redemption" (Ephesians 4:30).

W E SHOULD ALWAYS BE careful in what we do, and try to glorify God's name. It's important as Christians not to live in sin against God. We are regenerated by the Holy Spirit moving into our hearts. "For John baptized with water, but in a few days you will be baptized with the Holy Spirit" (Acts 1:5). "I baptize you with water for repentance. But after me will come one who is more powerful than I whose sandals I am not fit to carry. He will baptize you with the Holy Spirit and with Fire" (Matthew 3:11).

After being baptized, I started my new life at church as a "newborn baby", thirsty for God's word. I tried hard to learn God's word because it is so important. God's word is the Sprit and the life and gives you direction, comfort, healing, wisdom, peace, joy, courage, and encouragement. God's word is the best thing you can ever have. It is so important for you to grasp this fully. I was filled with joy as I was "transformed" by God's word living in me.

"For the word of God is living and active. Sharper than any double-edged sword, it penetrates even to dividing soul and spirit, joints and marrow; it judges the thoughts and attitudes of the heart" (Hebrews 4:12). I love to read the word of God daily. It is a habit I have that nourishes my heart, mind, and soul. I want to hear his voice through his word, so I can train my ears and heart to be more alert in his instruction for my life. Hearing his voice clearly helps me make the best decisions according to His will. "Today, if you hear his voice, do not harden your hearts" (Hebrews 4:7). By putting His word into practice, we can have "a Sabbath-Rest" in our heart.

Since becoming a new believer, I didn't miss a single Sunday sermon at my seminary school in the Church. Whenever and wherever I traveled, I would find a local church to attend on Sundays. Going to church allowed me to study, learn God's word and embrace God's love for me in Christ. I couldn't get enough of Him.

When I first started reading the Bible, despite my best efforts, it didn't always make sense to me. I found it dull, even though I knew from my pastor's teaching that reading the Bible daily would feed me spiritually. As I compared reading the Bible with reading other literature, I sometimes wanted to give up. I complained not being able to understand God's word. But blessed are those who are patient in reading the Bible. After three years of trying to read and understand the Bible, God's Holy Spirit taught me the message of the entire Bible in one week. This was amazing. Only the Holy Spirit can help us to understand His word. It is not by our own understanding, wisdom, intelligence, or knowledge, that we understand scripture. "The unfolding of your words gives light; it gives understanding to the simple" (Psalm 119:130). God made His words ALIVE to me. Now I love to read the Bible. I love to read it every day, to do God's will in my daily life. "Your word is a lamp to my feet and a light for my path" (Psalm 119:115). "How sweet are your words to my taste, sweeter than honey to my mouth" (Psalm 119:103).

In my new life, God wanted me to know Him, understand His word and experience a deeper relationship with Him. Every morning I would open my eyes and praise the Lord because I know His word can save me from all my affliction. "In the morning, O Lord, you hear my voice; in the morning, I lay my requests before you and wait in expectation" (Psalm 5:3). "To the Lord I cry aloud, and He answers me from His holy hill" (Psalm 3:4). Because I know "From the Lord comes deliverance. May your blessing be on your people" (Psalm 3:8). I would sing a song of praises to Him. "Praise the Lord, how good it is to sing praises to our God. How pleasant and fitting to praise him!" (Psalm 147:1). Daily praying and praising our Lord makes me very joyful and happy. "How can I repay the Lord for all his goodness to me? I will lift up the cup of salvation and call on the name of the Lord. I will fulfill my vows to the Lord in the presence of all his people" (Psalm 116: 12-14). I woke up every morning with a thankful attitude speaking in tongues for several minutes. When you do this, He reveals himself to you. My thankfulness and attitude came from my devotion to Jesus for His grace and mercy on me, my family, the church and all the nations.

I also went to the "Morning Prayer" meeting every morning with the pastors. During this meeting, the pastors gave a short daily message from the Bible.

I jumped into our church "Bible study" seminary every week. Here we sought to read and understand the truth of God's word. The District Leaders encouraged Grace and I to attend a weekly cell group. I was so thirsty for God's word. I hungered to fill up with His truths from the Bible. I think of the Bible as *"Best Ingredients Brewed Life Elements"* BIBLE. I attended a cell and life group for six months and felt God's love through my brothers and sisters in Christ. The district leader encouraged me to open my house for cell and life group studies and fellowship, so I hosted these studies after half a year of being in the Church. I was happy to even leave my house key with my district leader to continue to use my home as a fellowship place, even while our family was travelling. I know this house belongs to our Lord, who will take care of everything for us. I can feel the love from my family of brothers and sisters in Christ, floating up like fresh incense as worship and praise to God.

CHAPTER 16

I WENT FROM HAVING NO belief in God whatsoever, to being baptized by the Holy Spirit. After this, I was water baptized. After my first miracle of being graciously baptized by the Holy Spirit and in water, I was not prepared for another big miracle to happen to me in my life. One day in church, about two weeks after being saved, the pastor called my name. He called me and Grace to come to the platform. The pastor prophesied over us saying God would give us a miracle by the end of the month. At that time, I had no idea what this miracle could be. After two weeks, I found out that Grace was pregnant. We had tried to have a baby for seven to eight years after the birth of our first son without success.

So, on this special Sunday, shortly after being saved, my first fruit in Church would be a precious new baby boy, John, whom God promised to me through His servant's prophecy. If you believe in God and the Lord Jesus, you will have victory. Looking back, I know how important it is as a Christian to know and understand God's word as a "powerful engine" in your heart to be ignited. Put your faith in God and He will pour his blessings on you. Like the faith of the Centurion that Jesus told "Go! It will be done just as you believed it would," And his servant was healed at that very hour" (Matthew 8:13).

Also, in the Old Testament, Jehoshaphat stood and said to his people: "Have faith in the Lord your God and you will be upheld; have faith in his prophets and you will be successful" (2 Chronicles 20:20). In Second Peter, Peter also taught us that "For prophecy never had its origin in the will of man, but prophets, though human, spoke from

God as they were carried along by the Holy Spirit" (2 Peter 1:21). Your faith MUST be rooted in The Lord to believe in Him, His word, His prophecies, and His promises. Grace was pregnant after two weeks. Nine months later, our second child, John, was "born". How merciful God is to give this miracle to me, Grace, and our whole family. I am humbled by His lavish love for us.

After coming to the Lord, I felt the Holy Spirit call me to serve in the church. After about three months, I was assigned to wash all the dishes after the members' lunch. This was the last thing on earth, that I wanted to do. It was the first time my district leader asked me to do anything. I had to obey this calling, but I felt shame inside my heart. I endured dish duty for quite some time. Although I was embarrassed, I knew I should obey God's call to serve the church. Inside I was thinking of how much I hated this job, and I asked myself, "Do I really have to do this to be a Christian?" As I washed the dirty plates, bowls and cutlery, I reminisced about China. I remembered when I was treated like a "king" in Shanghai and was served so many delicious, gourmet foods. Now here I am serving the Lord as a dishwasher. But, this job really changed my heart and my life.

God gave me the opportunity to go to church and to serve in the lowest of positions. He also blessed me abundantly for my obedience. I see now that God was training me to be humble, by having me do the things I least wanted to do in my life. He can use you to do the small things and train you in "small beginnings" step by step for "big things" in your future. Through menial tasks, God is preparing you to be His good servant and warrior. As Jesus taught the master in the Bible "Whoever can be trusted with very little can also be trusted with much, and whoever is dishonest with very little will also be dishonest with much" (Luke 16:10). "Well done, good and faithful servant! You have been faithful with a few things; I will put you in charge of many things" (Matthew 25:23).

God can allow you to go through uncomfortable situations, with difficult people and He may do this to train you. I learned that to follow Christ, you sometimes have to suffer. In this suffering, you see that you are a child of God. We know Jesus and we know His resurrection power, but we also know we have to suffer with Him together for the Kingdom. So, I learned to humbly obey the requests of my pastors and district leaders in every opportunity to serve the Lord in His church. I learned to do whatever God wanted me to do even if the tasks were small and degrading. I cleaned the church hallways. I picked up litter on the ground etc. I was given various responsibilities. God opened my eyes to see what needed to be done at His church, and he gave me the desire, the strength, and the energy to get it done. Sometimes I would come to church and see that the faucets in the bathroom were dripping. So I would occasionally fix the plumbing. There were hundreds of people who went through the building on a Sunday and during the week, so the bathrooms were often quite a mess. Everything I did, I did unto the Lord. As much as I thought that the work was beneath me, I tried to imagine I was cleaning for the Lord to please Him.

The church hallways would often become messy with litter, so I would ensure the hallways were swept and vacuumed every Sunday. We wanted new people and the church family to know this place belonged to the Lord, and that we honored and maintained our place of worship of Him.

We seemed to grow in number and people flocked to the church to hear and receive more of our amazing God. The parking lot was sometimes chaotic with the rapid growth, so I often had to direct traffic to help families find parking safely and in an orderly fashion. We had many senior citizens in the congregation. Many of them were not able to drive anymore. I took on the responsibility of picking them up and bringing them to church, and then driving them home afterward. I often went without eating lunch until 3:30 pm each Sunday when I got home. I felt very blessed and rewarded to be able to do this. I got to know many of the older people. They have years of experience. They love the Lord and have served their families with much devotion. I take my good health and strength for granted sometimes, but when I help the seniors at our church, I am thankful I still have a strong body and mind and can still drive. Seeing life through their eyes, helps me appreciate what the Lord has given me.

Many new immigrants came to our Church drawn by the Holy

Spirit. I found the church congregation was growing both in number and in diversity. I was thankful to the Lord that he brought other nations to this church. I was happy to pick up new immigrants and give them a tour of the church facility. We offered them an orientation program to help them connect with the church members and become familiar with the church programs that were available. I remember when I first came to the U.S. as a new immigrant. I was lonely and miserable, but God sent people to show his love to me. I want to help these people feel God's love and care right away. He is a mighty God and cares about every detail of our lives.

We held many church events, reaching out to the community with the light and the love of the Lord. There was much to do to share God's truth to those who desperately needed God's compassion, mercy, grace, and forgiveness. I was so thankful the Lord did not forsake me or abandon me. <u>I knew God had rescued me from my darkness, so that I too could bring His light to others.</u> The members get excited about our church events. They love to eat together and fellowship during lunch time. They like to meet and go on adventures together. We explore the world as a group, and as a church family. We also go on overseas mission trips together to share the gospel to different countries.

We need our brothers and sisters in Christ. We are all one body, just different parts of the body. But we are all necessary and important for our Church body to grow in faith and in love. The Lord called me to organize church group events. He calls us to worship Him in community. The Lord reveals to us that we need to share life together as God's people, always encouraging each other and glorifying God with our love and support for each other. The Church group events are a fun way to bond with each other. It is a privilege to pray for people you enjoy being with and who become your very best friends. The enemy tries to defeat, discourage, destroy, and separate. We as believers need to stick together in Christ Jesus to pray for one another and be the Lord's hands and feet. The enemy wants us to be alone and isolated, so when he attacks us, we feel weak and have no one to turn to for help and support. He wants us to think we deserve our troubles or feel ashamed about our trials.

"Though one may be overpowered, two can defend themselves. A cord of three strands is not quickly broken" (Ecclesiastes 4:12). We should always be united in one body in Christ.

The Lord also called me to lead a church Bible study for years. It was a privilege to serve in this amazing ministry. The curious minds of the new believers with their passionate spirits blessed me as I would share the Lord's truths with them. While I am teaching adult Sunday school, Grace teaches children's Bible classes. She knows how important children are to Jesus. Mark 10:14 says "Let the little children come to me, and do not hinder them, for the kingdom of God belongs to such as these". Both of us feel so very blessed by having these opportunities to serve the Lord at the same time. I think of it as a "Double Portion Blessing" to my family. We were both blessed and learned much serving in these ministries. Mark 10:15 says "Truly I tell you, anyone who will not receive the kingdom of God like a little child will never enter it."

Sometimes members of our congregation would fall sick and be hospitalized. The Lord would call me to visit them and pray for their healing. The Lord is compassionate and powerful to heal. Like Jesus, who only does the will of the Father, I only wanted to do what God asked of me. Jesus gave them this answer: "I tell you the truth, the Son can do nothing by himself: he can do only what he sees his Father doing, because whatever the Father does the Son also does. For the Father loves the Son and shows him all he does. Yes, to your amazement he will show him even greater things than these" (John 5:19-20).

I was deeply blessed when I went to visit one of my sisters in Christ at the hospital. She needed a heart operation. She was very worried and dreaded the procedures the doctor told her prior to the operation. She was feeling it was the end of her life and worried that she might not be able to make it through the surgery. She cried quietly, broken, and hopeless. I just prayed by using God's word and comforted her, reassuring her that she would be totally healed this time, without a doubt. I told her God's stripes on the cross promised her healing. We marveled together at God's great power to "close the lion's mouths, and that Daniel walked out of the den without a scratch." After praying and when the operation was over, she knew, that she too would walk out of the hospital one day soon. The operation was successful, and God had given my sister in Christ a miracle.

It is a great reward to help others see themselves through God's eyes. God loves us through people, through our arms around them, through our smiles, our flowers, hot soup at the right time, and in the squeeze of a hand. Physical healing is amazing, but spiritual healing is the best miracle. Just like the woman at the well in the Bible was so transformed by a short conversation with Jesus, that she led a whole town to meet Jesus and to Salvation in Christ. (John 4:5-42)

I was honored and privileged to participate in Baptism Sundays at our church. What a celebration it is to share the symbolic moment of spiritual death to spiritual life. The Lord greatly blessed me in my role in this ministry. I often wonder why the Lord has chosen me to receive such privileges. I was in the baptism tank one Sunday when a young man gave his personal testimony. I was so touched by his love for the Lord and his complete surrender and trust in God. The Lord had carried him through a difficult time in his life because his parents had just gotten divorced. He wanted to end his life, but the Lord gave him the strength and the will to live despite his world crashing down around him. He has a brand-new life in Jesus now. His heart was once shards of broken glass, but God makes all things new again.

As people at the church chose to follow Christ, I felt the Lord call me to follow up with them. Salvation is the biggest and best miracle for anyone to experience. It was an honor and a privilege to visit them in their homes. When the Lord opens your eyes to the truth, you become a newborn baby. How refreshing it is to get to be with those who experience new life again for the first time as a renewed adult. It is a humbling experience to be around new believers in their new love relationship with the Lord. It is exciting and rewarding. The Holy Spirit is moving in the church, in their homes and in their hearts. Sometimes when I would visit their homes, I would help them get rid of any idol statues that they had in their possession. It was like being in war. We put on our armor and attacked the enemy. The enemy has no authority in our homes and lives. So, I helped these families kick them out. It was a freeing experience for them. It's like a thousand pounds being lifted off your shoulders. It's like chains wrapped around our ankles, being broken. They are free to walk and run their race for the Lord. We need to walk in the power of the Holy Spirit who gives us victory over sin, so that we may be free to worship Jesus with our lives and our hearts.

God's word is so powerful. It is alive and reveals God's nature, love, and purpose for us. I am always amazed at what God reveals to me as I read the Bible. God has called me to lead Bible studies for my church family. It is wonderful to dig deep into His word and grow in our relationship with Him as a group. When new believers are part of the Bible study, you are asked many great questions, that all levels of believers can learn from. Whatever the Lord asks me to do, I obey. I also went overseas to preach the gospel at different churches. God will use whatever you have for serving Him and His purposes. God wants to mature us and bring us to higher spiritual levels. The more I serve the Lord, the more humble and fearful I am of Him. If you do not serve Him, your pride and boasting will kill you. "I want to know Christ and the power of His resurrection and the fellowship of sharing in His sufferings, becoming like Him in His death, and so, somehow, attaining to the resurrection from the dead" as Paul taught us in the book of Philippians 3:10.

Chapter 17

WHEN I FIRST WENT to church, I didn't have much money. Each Sunday whenever the offering basket came to me, I would quickly pass it on, and I wouldn't give anything to the Lord. I was poor. I had no money to give. After some time, I felt very ashamed. Eventually I would give the Lord twenty dollars and sometimes fifty dollars in cash when the offering basket was passed to me. But God builds you up gradually not quickly. One day I was very fortunate and blessed to hear a sermon the pastor preached about the relationship between our faith and our tithe or offering. This teaching bothered me, and I felt it was the pastor's way of asking the congregation for more money. I didn't want to listen to his sermon, but suddenly, I felt "today I have to give the Lord some money". I felt the Holy Spirit tell me to give some money to the Lord.

I had just started a new company and didn't have any extra money left. I had to pay what I had into office rental fees. I had my family to support. As well, Grace's parents were visiting us for the first time in our small rented apartment, which was an additional financial burden to us. Grace was also pregnant, and I needed to buy more nutritious food for her, but clearly the Holy Spirit told me to give the Lord a cheque. I don't normally even carry a cheque book with me to church. But that day, I put my hand in my pocket and there was a cheque book in my pocket. This amazed me. God was doing things I couldn't understand. I didn't check with my wife first, who was standing beside me, and I wrote the cheque to the church for two hundred dollars. I felt so happy and joyful. Grace didn't know how much we were giving. Her parents were staying with us at the time and we were supporting them, so we didn't have extra money to give to the church.

When Grace found out, she was not very happy. I thought I made a mistake, so after discussing it with Grace, we decided to ask the pastor to give us the cheque back. But I never asked for it and I was disappointed in myself that I was unable to keep my promise to my wife. After a week, I totally forgot about giving the $200.00 cheque to the church. Three weeks later, I got a phone call from China. He had a container that had to be traded. He asked me to help him sell the container. I agreed to help him and made a phone call to see if I could sell this container. In that one call, I profited $7,000.00; the most money I had made by making a single phone call. I had to pinch myself because I thought I was dreaming. I gave the Lord $200.00 and He gave me $7,000.00. That was an incredible amount of money to me and my family. I obeyed the Holy Spirit and God blessed me abundantly. Our God is so faithful. I learned you can't out give God.

You just never know what God will do to bless you, but His words are true, and He is faithful. "Will a man rob God? Yet you rob me. But you ask, 'How do we rob you?' In tithes and offerings. You are under a curse-the whole nation of you-because you are robbing me. Bring the whole tithe into the storehouse, that there may be food in my house. 'Test me in this', Says the Lord Almighty, 'and see if I will not throw open the floodgates of heaven and pour out so much blessing that you will not have room enough for it' (Malachi 3: 8-10). This is an important commandment and promise from our lovely God to bless and prosper you abundantly in all aspects of your life. My faith had skyrocketed to great heights. My tithing from that time never stopped for one moment. I continued to obey the Holy Spirit and give tithes to the Lord. I trusted the Lord and He blessed me more than I could ever imagine. <u>He will build your faith up when you take action, and you will be blessed beyond belief</u>. "In the same way, faith by itself, if it is not accompanied by action, is dead" (James 2:17). So, you must have faith and then take action as per God's will, to fulfill His plans for your life.

Where does faith come from? "Consequently, faith comes from hearing the message, and the message is heard through the word about

Christ" (Romans 10:17). I still remembered a unique experience I had when I went overseas to share the gospel. In one of the small groups, that night, I shared about "tithing" to God as a Christian. After I finished my message, I drove back to the hotel. In the car on the way back, I heard a voice say, "your message is great, but you should go back to the small group to make a donation to a special member of your group, who needs it". Instantly I drove back to that house and gave what I had with me, $100 dollars. After leaving the house, I felt so peaceful and joyful. I was very thankful for God's word reminding me "your message of tithing should be finished with your action of donating this $100 to encourage all the small group members". As a Christian, we shouldn't only preach the gospel, we should act accordingly. Once again, "Faith by itself, if it is not accompanied by action, is dead" (James 2:17).

Therefore, if you want to grow your faith, you must be still and hear the message of the word of Christ, and take the opportunities to act on His word for you. God calls us to serve Him physically in our work, but God also calls us to worship Him with our finances. I think many Christians find this hard to do, but God richly blesses you when you fear, and worship Him freely with your finances, in truth and Spirit. He will bring wealth and honor and LIFE to you. As an unbelieving person, you might be richly blessed with wealth and honor, but you will not be blessed with eternal life and all the blessings that come with it, apart from Christ.

Chapter 18

B ACK WHEN I WAS in China, my English Literature professor from the U.S. asked each student one by one in the class for an "English name", so he didn't have to call us by our Chinese name. He found Chinese names sometimes difficult for him to remember or enunciate. Everyone gave the professor an English name, and at my turn, I instantly blurted out the name "Peter". I hadn't even given any thought to it. I didn't even know the meaning of such a name and or knew of anyone called by that name. It was not until later, that I was told that the name Peter was one of the people in the book called the Bible. At that time, I had never even heard about such a book. Some classmates liked this name while others did not. Some students even hated it –but whatever, I was not very concerned about it either way.

Ever since then, I go by the name Peter. Now, this reminds me of the story of when God called Abram out of his country to the land of Canaan. God changes his name from Abram to Abraham to bless him "as a father of many nations" to "make him very fruitful" in the land of Canaan – "a land of milk and honey" (Genesis 12:7). But the most important meaning of changing Abraham's name is that God chose Abraham as his royal child with His agape love and God established His covenant as an everlasting covenant with Abraham: the covenant of circumcision for Abraham to be Holy and set apart from the world -He belonged to God from that moment as the chosen one.

Nobody knew, but it was ten years later that this godly, prophesized name "Peter", which was miraculously given to me, made me very "fruitful". Little did I know, I would receive a harvest of "153 fish" in my seafood business. I could not have known this when I chose the name Peter for myself. It was a total mystery to me, why I chose this name, because I had no idea or plan to open a Seafood business after I moved to San Francisco. I was unable to understand God's will to give me such a name, until a miracle occurred in my fish business. This miracle happened shortly after I moved to San Francisco from Boston, where I pursued my master's degree at the City College of San Francisco. One day, while I was praying, I heard a voice saying, "you can open your own business and I will have someone invest in it." I couldn't believe what I was hearing. This happened just after my baptism at the Church and in my mind, I thought to myself, "I am not prepared for this". I didn't have money to make a business investment at the time, but rather was employed in one of the seafood companies locally. Working there helped me earn a living, shortly after graduating from university.

One morning I came to the office very early. There was no one there yet. I was all by myself. Since I had no keys to the door, I walked around the whole office complex building blessing and worshipping the Lord. I was praising Him and singing to our Lord, as I had been taught by my pastors at church. I felt very happy without any troubles or heavy burdens weighing on my heart. While I was singing and praising God, His glory and mercy fell over me. It was during my praising and worshipping, I heard this "gentle voice" in my ear saying, "I will send an investor, so you can start your own joint company and in two weeks you will encounter the investor." I was surprised to hear such a voice in my ear, but frankly I had a strong enough faith to believe God's word in the spirit: I was certain that it was indeed from our God. Just as I was receiving this in my spirit, my office colleague arrived with the key to open the office door.

I kept all this a secret in my heart and mind. I didn't even tell Grace. It is so important for us as Christians to have the "vision" kept in our hearts each time God reveals his plan to us and for us. When God tested Abraham at the region of Moriah on one of the mountains, to sacrifice his only son Isaac as a burnt offering, Abraham did not tell anyone about this commandment from God. He took only two servants with him to go to the mountain, and went without discussing anything with his wife Sarah. "The mouth of the righteous is a fountain of life, but violence overwhelms the mouth of the wicked" (Proverbs 10:11). "When words are many, sin is not absent, but he who holds his tongue is wise" (Proverbs 10:19). Yes, it is a great lesson for us to learn and we must have wisdom to keep our tongues still until God's prophecy is fulfilled. "Every prudent man acts out of knowledge, but a fool exposes his folly" (Proverbs 13:16).

Exactly two weeks after the time of this revelation, a person I had only chatted with one time before, knocked on my door. He said he was interested in starting a business with me and would like to invest in a company to buy fish from China. I couldn't believe my ears! I confirmed the information with him twice and miraculously funds were wired for the running of our new company. Just as the voice told me, this happened two weeks after hearing from the Lord. I worked together with this "silent partner" for three months without much contact.

During that time, I often went to church in the morning for a prayer meeting and then a short message from the pastors. One afternoon, as usual, I knelt down to pray. While I was praying, a breeze blew in and turned my open Bible to John Chapter four. I looked up and a drop of blood fell from the sky. It came from heaven. I was amazed and my whole body was shaking. I couldn't believe what I was seeing. A second drop of blood fell and landed on John 4:38. The drops of blood were in the shape of a heart. I didn't know the meaning behind the two drops of blood that fell from heaven, so I asked my pastor. At that time, my fishing company was not in good financial shape. The pastor said, "The blood means Jesus will cleanse your sins and God has given you a revelation for a healthy business".

After two years, I graciously and surprisingly, received a big order (like the 153 fish Peter caught in his net) from one of the fish companies ordering a large amount of frozen fish. This order translated into a profit of about one million dollars. This was completely amazing to me! I didn't know how Mr. Ed Lao could place such a large order. Why did he choose me? I did not quite understand it, since I only did one small business transaction with him prior to this big order. I wondered how he could so easily trust me with such a large order. Later, I learned he was also a Christian. How marvelous is God for pouring out His favor on me through this rare business opportunity? It was like Peter the fisherman in the Bible; the name I was called and had assigned myself years ago, in my college days. Having the name, Peter, was God's prophecy. It was a miracle and was both fruitful in my spirit and in my daily life. He has prepared all for you, just as Jesus told Peter "...go to the lake and throw out your line, take the first fish you catch; open its mouth and you will find a four-drachma coin" (Matthew 17:27B). God's prophecy is powerful, wonderful, beautiful, and amazing. John 4:38 later touched my heart profoundly in light of this reaping of abundant "fish" from my Lord. "I sent you to reap what you have not worked for. Others have done the hard work, and you have reaped the benefits of their labor." All this happened after I chose "Peter" to be my English name back in the day my English professor asked me to choose a name. **"And I tell you, you are Peter"** What a wonderful name and promise God gave to me, in giving me my new name "Peter". He blessed me as a "fisherman catching 153 fish".

God gave me this vision through the drops of this precious blood. He can give us visions that will reveal His purpose for us. We just need to be spiritually cleansed, sanctified, and molded so that we can receive His visions for us. It was promised to all men in the end times, that "Your young men will see visions" (Acts 2:17). He calls us to obey Him and follow His commands. He blessed me financially, so I could support the works of my church and help others that He calls me to help, like our church members and our families that are in need. My faith is tremendously growing day by day as I experience God's love through the signs and wonders that follow my family.

CHAPTER 19

GOD'S MIRACLES FOR US are always beyond our knowledge. They are sometimes even "irrational and ridiculous." It was during the starting point of my spiritual growth in God's word, when I was enthusiastic and zealous to serve our Beloved Lord, that I strangely found my physical body changing. It seemed like I was a young boy again, growing in height daily. Grace and some district leaders, as well as some brothers and sisters at our Church noticed a miraculous change in my height. At first, I was not aware of this growth, as I was nearly forty years old and it seemed physically impossible from a realistic standpoint to accept the fact that I had grown five inches! I couldn't believe it until the time I went back to Shanghai to visit my parents, who also noticed my amazing growth. This caused me to finally consult doctors and experts over the course of nearly three months to explain this strange phenomenon. Looking back, I accept this as God's grace. It was a "double portion of blessing", which was afforded to me, as my physical growth seemed to occur in conjunction with the spiritual growth I was also experiencing. It isn't until now, that I finally feel normal in all aspects of my life. My height is stable now and the condition of my health is very good. All glory belongs to our Lord who performs all kinds of miracles for His purposes for me and for you, beyond what our limited human minds can comprehend.

In the same instance, I could understand the uncertainness and doubt Sarah had for God's promise to her and Abraham when God promised them a son at Abraham's very old age of one hundred. Sarah's response was to "laugh to herself as she thought and said she was worn out and her master Abraham was too old to have a baby." But in contrast, God said to them: "Is anything too hard for the Lord?" (Genesis 18:14). In the New Testament, Jesus speaks to His disciples about the rich entering the kingdom of God: "Jesus looked at them and said, 'with man this is impossible, but not with God; all things are possible with God'" (Mark 10:27).

As God's children, we are thankful and pray in everything and for everything as we increase in both the understanding of His word and the interceding of the Holy Spirit. Our faith needs growing, and our heart should be opened widely to receive God's love. We need to trust His directions, because His plans are always the best plans. "Therefore, let us leave the elementary teachings about Christ and go on to maturity," (Hebrews 6:1A) to live in the Holy Spirit. You must face trials of many kinds, but you don't need to be afraid of anything, as you know, our faith must go through all kinds of tests to become mature and complete. "Blessed is the man who perseveres under trial, because when he has stood the test, he will receive the crown of life that God has promised to those who love Him" (James 1:12).

Fear of the Lord is the beginning of wisdom. We can ask God for wisdom, and he will give it to us. "And Jesus grew in wisdom and stature, and in favor with God and men" (Luke 2:52).

One Sunday morning, when I was a new Christian, as we were worshipping and praising the Lord in song in the sanctuary, the senior pastor pointed to me with a gleam in his eye. He looked directly into my eyes. I was not prepared for this look. I did not know him, and he didn't know my name either at that time. He used his hand to call me out of the congregation and forward. He called on me to be a servant and usher for passing out the cups and bread for Holy Communion. My whole body became hot the moment my eyes locked onto the pastor's eyes. He grabbed my hand praying for me in the name of Jesus and led me to the front of the church. From that moment on, I served the Holy Communion cups every week, honoring the precious blood of Jesus Christ and the "Bread of Life". We honor Jesus' blood as our new life. "Therefore, brothers, since we have confidence to enter the Most Holy Place by the blood of Jesus, by a new and living way opened for us through the curtain, that is, his body, and since we have a great priest over the house of God, let us draw near to God with a sincere heart in full assurance of faith, having our hearts sprinkled to cleanse us from a guilty conscience and having our bodies washed with pure water" (Hebrews 10:19-22).

We still serve today at the church every Sunday. I never want to miss an opportunity to serve the Lord. I am there at every service at 10:00 am. One time I needed to travel to Boston. I specifically booked my flight to return home in time for Holy Communion. It's not really our senior pastor conducting this, but rather the Holy Spirit is present and leading this every Sunday. We should be very reverent and humble, and honor Our Lord with all our mind, body, and soul as living sacrifices to our God. "Therefore, I urge you, brothers, in view of God's mercy, to offer your bodies as living sacrifices, holy and pleasing to God - this is your spiritual act of worship. Do not conform any longer to the pattern of this world, but be transformed by the renewing of your mind. Then you will be able to test and approve what God's will is - his good, pleasing and perfect will" (Romans 12:1-3). "This is my body, which is for you; do this in remembrance of me; this cup is the new covenant in my blood; do this, whenever you drink it, in remembrance of me" (1 Corinthians 11:24-25).

God loves us so much, we need to prepare our hearts to fear, honor and respect Him, and to "proclaim the Lord's death till he comes". Have you ever experienced the power of Jesus Christ upon you at Holy Communion, the holy time of meeting? Have you ever seen the glory of our Lord embracing you in His agape love? The Lord will reveal His Spirit and appear to you in His glory to sustain you through your problems and heal all kinds of sickness. How wonderful to be with God in His glory during Holy Communion! Just like Peter's experience when he said to Jesus: "Lord, it is good for us to be here" (Matthew 17:4).

CHAPTER 20

WHEN YOU ARE IN the spiritual "baby stage", it is common to pray and ask God for what you want. God loves to listen to your prayers and give you what you want, according to His will, if you delight in Him. "And I will do whatever you ask in my name, so that the Son may bring glory to the Father. You may ask me for anything in my name, and I will do it" (John 14:13-14). God will bless you so much as a baby Christian after you are baptized and are following His path for you. My favorite Scripture as a new Christian is: "Ask and it will be given to you; seek and you will find; knock and the door will be opened to you. For everyone who asks, receives; he who seeks, finds; and to him who knocks, the door will be opened" (Matthew 7:7-8).

I asked for a son, and in five years, God gave me one. I asked for a car, and he gave me two. I asked for a house within a five-minute drive to the Church. As I boldly prayed in His presence, he graciously answered my prayer by giving me a beautiful house exactly a five-minute drive to the Church. "God gives you the desires of your heart when you delight in him" (Psalm 37:4). "The boundary lines have fallen for me in pleasant places; surely I have a delightful inheritance" (Psalm 16:6). God will provide what you need, but not necessarily what you want. All earth belongs to our Lord and He can be our refuge and rock to lean on, but "Unless the Lord builds the house, its builders labor in vain. Unless the Lord watches over the city, the watchmen stand guard in vain". We are best served if we not only pray for what we need, but also for what God wants for us.

We first lived in an apartment when we moved to San Francisco. It was a small two-bedroom apartment. It had a small deck that looked out onto the visitor parking lot. Grace did her best to make our home comfortable. She bought beautiful drapery, toss pillows in bright jewel tones and elegant pieces to furnish our humble apartment. Most of the time the furnishings and decor she purchased, were on sale. We had to be very careful with what we spent, because of our meager budget. We desired to live in a bigger space, so our son and future children could have a big back yard, and their own bedrooms. We wanted to give our son the very best life. We had to take him to a nearby park to play since we had no backyard. It would have been great if we could have three bedrooms, a garage for our car and a yard with some rose bushes and a flower garden. Our children could play in the back yard if we had one. Grace and I would look longingly at the beautiful homes in the area. We would get excited when we saw one for sale, but it was just a pipe dream to purchase our own home. We had not saved up for a down payment and we were just trying to make ends meet and pay our bills. We bought a second-hand bike for our first son Simon. We often checked out garage sales to see if we could find treasures for Simon. Thankfully, God sent one of my church sisters, Chunhua Chen, to graciously give us all her second-hand clothes, toys, shoes, etc. God is so generous and faithful. Since then, our two families have become great friends and the best spiritual partners.

We often ate rice and vegetables for breakfast, lunch, and dinner. We would splurge on chicken and beef occasionally. Meat and seafood were expensive and a luxury for us.

One day a sister at church asked me if I wanted to buy her house. I told her I didn't have any money to buy her house, since I had just started my business. I had no money at all. Sister Biyu was persistent however. She would follow me around on Sunday mornings at Church. "Where is your house" I asked? She gave me directions to her house after one Sunday service. The distance from her house to the church was less than I expected; even less than what I prayed for. It was only two minutes away. I began to think about how convenient it would be to live and go to Church every Sunday from her house. She told me she had a dream that I moved into her house. She wanted me to be the one to buy her house. "Really?" I said. But "I have no intentions of buying your house". Every time I would see her, she would tell me the same thing. My response was always the same, "I have no money." After one month, she said again "Brother, you must buy my house, I will sell it cheaply to you". I said, "How much will you sell it to me for, one dollar?" She said "No, no…I want to move to a bigger house, and the market value for my house is $300,000.00. I will give it to you for $200,000.00." "Really?" I exclaimed. "Why would you do that?" I asked. But once again I had to tell her, "I don't even have the down payment for it".

Sister Biyu's home was quite large. She had four bedrooms. There were large windows in the front that had a beautiful view of the palm trees that lined the homes across the street. There were beautiful rose bushes planted in the front of the house and both the front and back yards were meticulously landscaped with seven different fruit trees planted. There was a double garage and a long driveway that could park four more cars. The kitchen had just been renovated. It had pristine white cabinets with stainless steel knobs and quartz counters in cream with grey flecks. The floors were a tumbled marble tile in the kitchen, and hardwood in a hickory sunset color in the dining room. The living room had carpet in subtle colors of creams and soft greys. The walls were painted in soft white colors and a beautiful tablet hung on the wall that read "Christ is King of the Household." We could not dream of owning a home like hers. But the Lord is generous and has new mercies for us every morning.

That night, my first container of frozen seafood from China arrived and I traded it for a profit of $25,000. There was my down payment! Before that container arrived, I had the same dream three consecutive nights in a row. I dreamt Grace and Simon were following me, carrying many things, to Biyu's house. The Lord was confirming to me that He was choosing this blessed home for me and my family, according to His perfect will and timing. This fulfilled my sister's dream as well. I realized this house was reserved for us to glorify His name. In our new home, in the past twenty years, many people have come to Jesus, and incredible miracles happened to brothers and sisters in Christ. God's word and His Spirit have been manifested in my cell groups, etc. The

Holy Spirit is moving in our hearts. As our cell groups grow and connect people, more lives will be blessed. When you pray, God will use your household in a mighty way, in his perfect timing. His love is floating through each member to the outside world as salt and light. He always has the best plans for us.

One day when I was walking down the street, handing out gospel flyers, I met a man named Andrew Ai. I brought him to my cell and life group and to Church on Sunday. He was very poor both financially and physically. He and his family prayed, feared, trusted, and obeyed the Lord. They never missed one fellowship meeting. "Let us hold unswervingly to the hope we profess, for he who promised is faithful. And let us consider how we may spur one another on toward love and good deeds. Let us not Give up meeting together, as some are in the habit of doing, but let us encourage one another - and all the more as you see the Day approaching" (Hebrews 10:23-25).

They prayed for a car, a house, and a child. Within five years, God gave them everything they asked for. Why? Because they were very obedient to God's plan for their lives and they showed it through their actions. They were so blessed because they served the people at Church. I always use God's word to teach them. Spiritually, they grew so fast and they are now cell group leaders of our church. So many people are being helped through prayer. So many issues and problems are being resolved without explanation. We can only thank God for His special and gracious help. Our God is awesome! All things are possible with Him. "Ask and it will be given to you; seek and you will find; knock and the door will be opened to you. For everyone who asks receives; he who seeks finds; and to him who knocks, the door will be opened. Which of you, if his son asks for bread, will give him a stone? Or if he asks for a fish, will give him a snake? If you, then, though you are evil, know how to give good gifts to your children, how much more will your Father in heaven give good gifts to those who ask him!" (Matthew 7:7-11).

First, I encourage you to read God's word, go to church and receive His word for you in the teaching, during the sermon. Then seek to join a cell and life group and develop the habit of daily repentance, praising and worshipping Him. The Holy Spirit will help you have self-control, if you are intentional about walking with God. If you have the gift of "speaking in tongues", do this for at least half an hour every day. Ask the Holy Spirit to help you apply God's truth in your life every day.

When we know the truth, we should act based on the truth. The truth will set you free from any bondage. If we have true faith (hearing from the word of the Lord, Jesus Christ), we must act on our faith immediately, without delay. God desires us to obey His calling upon us to give and serve in His Church. "Do not merely listen to the word, and so deceive yourselves. Do what it says" (James 1:22). "Everyone who hears these words of mine and puts them into practice is like a wise man who built his house on the rock" (Matthew 7:24). Through God, we are all wise builders in the Lord's Kingdom.

CHAPTER 21

EACH WEEK WE HAD a cell and life group in our home. During our cell and life group, many miracles happened. The most important miracle was one involving two couples. Both couples had been trying to have a baby for a long time but were not able to conceive. They tried for children for about ten years. We prayed for them regularly for two years. It seemed quite hopeless. There is a parable of a "persistent widow" whose plea was finally answered by the judge. The story in the Bible teaches that we should continue to pray without ceasing, and that we should never give up until our prayers are answered, according to our Lord's will for us.

One night after our group meeting, we were having refreshments and God gave me a stunning vision. I started to see one of my sisters with a shining glory around her stomach. When I spoke to her, I told her what God had impressed on my heart. His profound and prophesized words for her "This week you will be pregnant" rolled off my lips. "You're crazy" she said. I responded, "I know that we prayed for two years and we didn't see any movement from God, but tonight I saw a vision. God surrounded you with His glory." The other sister said, "what about me? I have been praying too. Is God going to give me a child?" I did not see a vision for her, but God ordained me to prophesy, and I told her she would get pregnant also based on her faith in the Lord. Two weeks passed by and at the same time, at the same place, both sisters very happily told me they were pregnant! What an amazing miracle performed by our Lord! Sometimes, we are impatient in waiting for our answers and we sometimes even give up praying. Our faith diminishes without our knowledge, but you know what? It is at that very moment God's miracles are suddenly given to you because "Hope deferred makes the heart sick, but a longing fulfilled is a tree of life" (Proverbs 13:12).

After years of prayer, God fulfilled the dreams of both sisters. We continued to pray for these ladies. What was also shocking to me, was that they gave birth only one day apart. One had a girl, the other had a boy. This is only something God could have done. They themselves had been touched by God due to their obedience in prayer and meeting in the small group every week. These two couples were not extra-ordinary in any way, they were just very obedient to God and had pure loving hearts towards the people God put in their lives. They lived their lives according to God's word. God loves them so much and gave them both the desires of their hearts.

Since then, I found I have a special gift of praying for women who desire to have children. God has used me to pray for eight other couples with whom it also seemed impossible for them to conceive children. Eventually, all the couples got pregnant and God answered their prayers with children. God is so amazing and kind. Only through Him the impossible becomes possible. We give Him all the glory for the work He did in this cell and life group. God can use me, and anybody who clings to Him and is obedient to Him. These miracles amazed and encouraged all the members of our cell and life group and the members in our church. You may use your spiritual gifts to help others and as you give of your gifts, gifts will be given to you.

CHAPTER 22

I T WAS ABOUT SIX months after I was water baptized, that we first opened our home to our church family, so we could study God's word together. There were about twenty of us that met at our house every Wednesday evening to share scripture, praise the Lord and fellowship. I was very excited to host this cell group. I was inspired by the Lord and longed to serve Him in this capacity. I desired to meet with my brothers and sisters in Christ to worship and praise the Lord.

One Wednesday night after tidying our home, before the guests arrived, I stood outside my house looking at my rose garden. There were many roses that bloomed, and I was watering the bushes. I was so happy, watering the beautiful roses God had blessed us with. There were red, pink, white and yellow roses. As I was admiring God's art work, I fell to the ground. I didn't slip on anything, in fact I almost felt pushed. The thorns in the rose bushes made deep scratches all over my back and I was bleeding. I also hit my head on the concrete edge of my garden. I felt faint for about five minutes. After I recovered, I stood up and I was still feeling so happy. My cell and life group came over and we had a great gathering just sharing God's word and praising Him in song. I gave my testimony to the group that night. They were all amazed and we gave God all the glory that I wasn't seriously hurt. Looking back, I think that sometimes when you are on fire for the Lord, the enemy wants to attack you. I realized I didn't have to worry about the enemy, because God is always watching and protecting me. He always saves me from dangerous situations, despite the enemy's efforts. I'm so thankful that God is sovereign and in control all the time. I know God's angels were there to protect me from the fall. This night made me think of this verse: "He will command his angels concerning you, and they will lift you up in their hands, so that you will not strike your foot against a stone" (Psalm 91:11-12).

CHAPTER 23

ANOTHER TIME, WE WERE in the kitchen preparing delicious cookies and Chinese food for the cell group before they came over. Grace and I were working and chatting away in the kitchen before the cell group arrived. John, our beautiful two-year old son, was in the living room by himself, playing with his toys. Grace and I were chopping up vegetables and cooking, when suddenly, we heard a big thud, like something fell. We heard some crying, so we rushed to the living room looking for John. He was nowhere to be found. We could still hear the crying as we frantically searched for him. We finally found him lying on the ground in the backyard. He had fallen out the living room window. We were on the first floor and we didn't know how he fell and ended up in the backyard. John must have stood on the couch and opened the window and fell through, onto the cement in the backyard. Grace and I were horrified at what had happened and we didn't know what to do. John was lying on the ground also terrified and crying. We immediately called 911 and they sent an ambulance to our house. As we rode in the back of the ambulance with John, we were so scared and terrified about what would happen to our precious boy. During the ride in the ambulance, we pleaded with the Lord to have mercy on our son. John was our first fruit prophesied by our pastor when I first came to the Lord. He is the blessing we received from the Lord when we first joined this church.

We were sitting in the emergency room wondering the worst. Did he hurt his neck, or his spine? Is there internal bleeding in his brain? Is he going to be ok? He was just lying there crying. He couldn't talk yet.

We were so worried, but we continued to pray and pray. The doctor said if he damaged his spine, he could be paralyzed. We were extremely stressed, but in our anguish, we continued to pray for John. After the longest one and a half hours of our lives, and after a thorough medical examination of John, our son came out of the hospital without a single scratch or signs of any damage. The Lord was merciful and saved John from getting hurt when he fell. We were so thankful to God for this miracle. We wept in thankfulness knowing God had spared John and us from devastation and tragedy. God touched our hearts with His mercy for John. We give God all the glory for saving our son that day, which was again just before our cell and life group meeting.

Once more this showed me that when you have strong intentions to serve the Lord, the enemy will want to stop you with his evil plots and schemes. "Your enemy the devil prowls around like a roaring lion looking for someone to devour. Resist him, standing firm in the faith, because you know that the family of believers throughout the world is undergoing the same kind of suffering" (1Peter 5:8-9). The enemy doesn't want to release us from his grip, but I choose to cling to and depend on the Lord's grace, which is sufficient for me.

Thanks to God, our Lord Jesus prays for us, as He told Simon Peter: "Simon, Simon, Satan has asked to sift you as wheat. But I have prayed for you, Simon, that your faith may not fail. And when you have turned back, strengthen your brothers" (Luke 22:31-32). It is our Lord who is our Savior "To rescue us from the hand of our enemies, and to enable us to serve him without fear in holiness and righteousness before all our days" (Luke 1:74-75). What a great promise from God to us!

Chapter 24

A BOUT A YEAR LATER, we had another cell group meeting which also included district leaders. There were about fifty people in attendance. We were all going together on a field trip to tour a campus. It was a warm evening with a cool breeze. The air was filled with chatter and the buzz of excitement. Since there were many people going, we decided to take our van instead of our small Toyota Corolla. Usually I drive the van, however, we needed extra vehicles, so I planned to drive a few people in my small car and one of my new brothers in Christ was going to take a group of friends in my van. John usually rode in his car seat in the van. He was almost three years old and was joyfully anticipating the ride. He was getting cuter by the day, and the days were going so fast. I was the one who normally drove and was usually the one who buckled John into his car seat. John was securely buckled into the seat on the driver's side. Excited to get our adventure started, the driver used all his force to slide the van door shut. Unfortunately, he didn't see that John's small hand was between the frame of the van and the van door. I was five feet away and saw my son's hand crumple like paper as the van door slammed shut.

We were all crying, especially John as he must have been in excruciating pain. All the cell and life group members witnessed this accident. We didn't think his hand could be saved, because the driver pushed the door closed so hard. We all stood there in shock, but prayed fervently for the Lord to have mercy on John. We immediately called on God to help restore John's hand. "When I called, you answered me; you greatly emboldened me" (Psalm 138:3). All the church group members were holding their hands together in one spirit calling and crying for the Lord to show His mercy to John. John is such a "blessing from God" to our family. "The Lord will keep you from all harm - he will watch over your life; the Lord will watch over your coming and going both now and forevermore" (Psalm 121:7-8), we declared. As we were praying, we witnessed his crushed fingers and palm transform and completely restored. It was miraculous! The only sign that anything had even happened to his hand were some red spots on his skin. Not a single bone was broken.

There must have been an angel covering John's hand in protection, much like Abraham as he was about to kill his son as a sacrifice to God. The angel sent by the Lord stopped Abraham from striking down on his son with the knife, and provided Abraham with another sacrifice. Protecting John's precious, tiny hand in this unfortunate mishap is something only an angel from the Lord could have done. We really thank the Lord for his amazing protection throughout our lives. "The Lord watches over you - the Lord is your shade at your right hand; the sun will not harm you by day, nor the moon by night" (Psalm 121:5-6). Even though we can't see the Lord as he protects us, we know He is always there watching over us and helping us when we call to him. God sends angels ahead of us to protect us.

During our cell and life group meetings many things happened, but all was under the control of the Almighty God. He showed His love to His people. Many miracles happened. Everyone enjoyed God's word and being surrounded by God's love. When we went on missionary trips overseas, I gave the keys to my house to my district leaders, so we could continue to allow others to use our home for Bible studies, cell, life group meetings and prayer meetings. God has blessed our house and many people are continuing to be touched and changed by God's Spirit and power. God is rewarding them and giving them the desires of their hearts.

If you do not yet attend a cell and life group, I encourage you to take prompt action to be united in one family with brothers and sisters in God's love. Your life will be renewed and richly blessed as your faith is rooted and built up on the foundation of God's words. "The rain came down, the streams rose, and the winds blew and beat against that house; (your faith in God's word), yet it did not fall, because it had its foundation on the rock of God's word" (Matthew 7:25).

CHAPTER 25

ONE OF OUR NEIGHBORS, Yuan, was always very busy. She was a believer who took care of both her grandchildren and her dogs. She was always busy cooking and cleaning. Over a period of time we had become her best friends. One day I prophesied that Yuan shouldn't work so hard. Our whole home group prayed over her. Then one night around midnight, I received a phone call from her. "Peter, please come to my house, I have a very severe headache", she said. Grace and I went over to her place right away. We found her lying on the sofa and the color of her skin was a very pale gray. We called 911 and prayed for God to heal her illness.

No one was with Yuan except for one of her grandsons. All of her family was overseas, so we went with her to the hospital. We had to sign permission papers on behalf of her family. As I watched and prayed over her, I realized it was the first time in my life I had ever stayed awake for thirty hours straight. The Lord must have sustained me during this time. I called her daughter in Hong Kong right away telling her about her mom's situation. I told her that her mom was in a very serious coma. Yuan's daughter flew home right away, but Yuan died before her daughter arrived at the hospital. God used Grace and I to warn Yuan not to work so hard. "Come to me (Jesus), all you who are weary and burdened, and I will give you rest. Take my yoke upon you and learn from me, for I am gentle and humble in heart, you will find rest for your souls. For my yoke is easy and my burden is light" (Matthew 11:28). "Be still, and know that I am God" (Psalm 46:10); and "Praise be to the Lord, to God our Savior, who daily bears our burdens" (Psalm 68:19).

The Lord's word came to Zerubbabel: "Not by might nor by power, but by my Spirit" (Zechariah 4:6), to fulfill His works for us according to His will. As the chosen children, "Let us then approach the throne of grace with confidence, so that we may receive mercy and find grace to help us in our time of need" (Hebrews 4:16).

Sometimes, we are too busy to take the time to rest in the Lord and listen to his voice, so we know the right way to live our lives. Sometimes, we use our own wisdom and knowledge to pursue our dreams without asking God to guide our heart. The prophet Amos describes "Not a famine of food or a thirst for water, but a famine of hearing the words of the Lord. We (men) will stagger from sea to sea and wander from north to east, searching for the word of the Lord, but they will not find it" (Amos 8:11-12). "Man is a mere phantom as he goes to and from: He bustles about, but only in vain; he heaps up wealth, not knowing who will get it" (Psalm 39:6). As Jesus teaches us "therefore I tell you, do not worry about your life, what you will eat or drink; or about your body, what you will wear. Is not life more important than clothes? Look at the birds of the air; they do not sow or reap or store away in barns, and yet your heavenly Father feeds them. Are you not much more valuable than they?" (Matthew 6:25-26). "What good will it be for a man if he gains the whole world, yet forfeits his soul? Or what can a man give in exchange for his soul?" (Matthew 16:26). "But remember the Lord your God, for it is He who gives you the ability to produce wealth" (Deuteronomy 8:18). We need to wait patiently for the Lord; he will surely turn to us in our prayers. We need to "Seek first His Kingdom and His righteousness, and all these things will be given to you as well. Therefore, do not worry about tomorrow, for tomorrow will worry about itself. Each day has enough troubles of its own" (Matthew 6:33-34). We should learn as in our Lord's prayer, that we need also to ask and request God to "give us today our daily bread" (Matthew 6:11).

Sometimes God will use you to warn others to cherish their lives and to be careful with their time and strength. Sometimes God places us in the lives of those whose families are not there for them. We as Christian believers, need to become a family and meet the needs of our brothers and sisters in Christ. We are God's children here to show

His love to others in our daily lives, and not here just to be "One Day Christians" on Sunday in Church. "When someone is hungry and we give him something to eat; when someone is thirsty and we give him something to drink; when someone is a stranger and we invite him into our home; when someone needs clothes and we clothe him; when someone is sick and we look after him, when someone is in prison and we come to visit him," (Matthew 25:34-36) "The King will reply, 'Truly I tell you, and whatever you did for one of the least of these brothers and sisters of mine, you did for me'" (Matthew 25:40).

Thankfully, Yuan was baptized one and a half months before she died. Knowing that she gave her heart to the Lord brought much comfort to me and to her family. She is now resting in Jesus' arms in heaven.

As district leaders, we shepherd the flock. We must minister and come to the aid of those who have deep needs and are badly wounded. We need to show up and protect, help, and guide our sheep in the truth, love, and spirit of our God. It is our duty to help our brothers and sisters in Christ, when God calls us to.

Cell and life groups are a wonderful way to enrich our lives. These groups are a great practical way to grow together spiritually as we study His word and apply His truths to our lives. "He is like a tree planted by streams of water, which yields its fruit in season and whose leaf does not wither. Whatever he does prospers" (Psalm 1:3). There are thirty members in our cell and life group. We worship, and praise the Lord in song. We pray, fellowship and trust each other as one big family in Christ. We try and do everything according to His word and will. We practice "speaking in tongues" as "our payers in the Holy Spirit to keep ourselves in God's love waiting for the mercy of our Lord Jesus Christ to bring us to eternal life" (Jude: 20-21). When we need help from our Lord, we pray, and miracles happen when all our requests and expectations are surrendered to the Lord.

CHAPTER 26

THE CHURCH WAS IN the planning stages of building a Disciple Centre. We had an architect in our church family and he was asked to quote the job. After reviewing his quotation, I noticed he was going to profit quite a sum. I called him on this and he became angry and defensive. He left the church and we lost the only person fit to possibly tackle this huge project. No one wanted to touch this job. It was like a "hot potato". The Senior Pastor said "Peter, since you caused him to leave, you will build this Centre". I felt my face go flush and my neck was burning hot. What did I know about constructing a 20,000-square foot facility? I had absolutely no experience, expertise or knowledge of such an undertaking.

The most difficult time I had serving the Lord was when my pastor asked me to build this huge facility (Disciple Centre). This was a very tough job for me. I knew nothing about construction or building design. I don't know why God asked me to do this. This project was not only for our church, but it was also for believers from other countries, who would have the opportunity to be discipled in our church. I felt it was important for me to take on this task, but I had no wisdom or knowledge of how. It's like "trying to teach a cow to play the piano": It was all nonsense to me. I didn't even know where or how to begin. So, I did the only thing I knew to do, I fell to my knees and gave it to the Lord. If I were to build this facility, it would only be through His strength and wisdom.

The enemy did not want Shiloh Church to build a Disciple Centre. He attacked us on various fronts. It is a terrifying experience when you have an evil spirit come against you. Grace was very worried. During the process, from the beginning to its completion, we believe God was with us. Sometimes, we suffered a lot physically and spiritually. We hired new builders to work on the project. One of the builders was new in his faith. He had many questions. His faith was not firmly rooted in God's word. Our hopes of success were threatened as the builder and his wife, were causing big problems. One night after working on the construction site, they had a big argument. His wife warned us not to encourage him to serve the Lord. She even threatened suicide if he continued to work on the construction of the Disciple Center. Another night she fainted, in her attempts to stop her husband from working on the site. We often felt like just giving up, but knew we had to continue despite all the spiritual opposition. Sometimes my family was under persecution for no reason, due to the misconceptions of a few brothers and sisters in Christ. "Many are the foes who persecute us, but I have not turned from your statutes" (Psalm 119:157).

Grace and I called on God to help us get through this tough situation. We believed the Lord's promise from His faithful and living word that "We have come to share in Christ if indeed we hold firmly till the end the confidence we had at first" (Hebrews 3:14). We bowed down to God to seek wisdom on how to solve this dilemma and God graciously showed us the best way. He showed us to first pray for this builder's wife. We knew that God would give us the wisdom and the knowledge because "...the Lord gives wisdom, and from his mouth come knowledge and understanding. He holds victory in store for the upright, he is a shield to those whose walk is blameless, for he guards the course of the just and protects the way of his faithful ones" (Proverbs 2:6-8). Finally, God indicated to us that the best way to comfort his wife, was with His precious word from the Holy Bible.

The facility was half finished. God gave Grace much wisdom. She prayed that God would soften the heart of the builder's wife, so she would allow him to build this center for future disciples. Grace was a mentor to her. We didn't know how to help her, but somehow, by God's grace, we were able to convince her to support her husband in keeping the project alive. If it is God's will, and if you commit your plans to the

Lord, they will succeed. "Commit to the LORD whatever you do and he will establish your plans" (Proverbs 16:3).

I didn't know how to build this "Disciple Center", but I devoted all my efforts to this very daunting project. The project was finished after about three years. I was feeling very proud of myself for persevering through all the "suffering", but I give all the glory to our amazing God. "I can do all things through Christ who strengthens me" (Philippians 4:13). I am just a work of His hand and can do nothing apart from Him. God has done much through me, but the main thing I learned is that whether I have little or much, I need to give it to the Lord and He will do great and mighty things with it. Just like when the small boy with five small barley loaves and two small fish gladly offered them to Jesus and our Lord miraculously turned them into enough "heavenly food" to feed thousands. He even had enough left over to fill twelve baskets (John 6:5-12). Use all your wisdom, knowledge, and wealth for Jesus and He can perform great miracles for you which will also benefit others.

I believe we can find many ways in our churches, our communities and even in our daily lives to serve the Lord with what we have. When we serve the Lord, we will be richly and abundantly blessed. He will bless you physically, emotionally, and even financially. When you seek God's Kingdom first, you will be very satisfied. There is nothing better than serving the Lord.

God can use your smile, gestures and even your very breath to serve other people, including your neighbors, family, and friends. Even if we only have a small knowledge of the Bible, we need to serve God by mobilizing His word in our lives daily. When people see us they will recognize us, as Jesus' disciples and give the glory to Him. Our names will be written in heaven as a most glorious reward. "However, do not rejoice that the spirits submit to you, but rejoice that your names are written in heaven" (Luke 10:20).

There are many ways to serve the Lord. As Jesus said to His disciples, "The harvest is plentiful but the workers are few. Ask the Lord of the harvest, therefore, to send out workers into his harvest field" (Matthew 9:37-38). You may find there are people around you "harassed and helpless, like sheep without a shepherd". You ARE a shepherd just as was the Samaritan woman, whose testimony about Jesus brought salvation to her town. In Jesus, we command ourselves Not to receive God's grace in vain but to use God's grace in us to sow and harvest more souls.

It was a real miracle to see God help and use me as well as others to successfully complete the 20,000-square foot Disciple Center in three years. The Center was constructed and built to honor God. The facility was designed to disciple the Lord's people in our church and His people outside our church. I pray for this great and blessed building that the Lord miraculously granted. I pray and hope that this beautifully finished and finely constructed building will be well used as a place for God's agape love to benefit many of His disciples. "By wisdom a house is built, and through understanding it is established; through knowledge its rooms are filled with rare and beautiful treasures" (Proverbs 24:3-4). I often lift my hands praying in the name of Jesus to bless this "Disciple Center" building, that it be filled with God's love, truth, peace, kindness, wisdom, knowledge, and that people would grasp His Holiness.

"How lovey is your dwelling place, O Lord Almighty! My soul yearns, even faints, for the courts of the Lord; my heart and my flesh cry out for the living God. Even the sparrow has found a home, and the swallow a nest for herself, where she may have her young - a place near your altar, O Lord Almighty, my King, and my God. Blessed are those who dwell in your house; they are ever praising you... Better is one day in your courts than a thousand elsewhere; I would rather be a doorkeeper in the house of my God than dwell in the tents of the wicked. For the Lord God is a sun and shield; the Lord bestows favor and honor; no good thing does he withhold from those whose walk is blameless. O Lord Almighty, blessed is the man who trusts in you" (Psalm 84:1-4; 10-12).

Yes, don't wait another minute, but rather direct your steps to our Lord's Holy Church, "For there the Lord bestows in his blessing, even life forevermore" (Psalm 133:3B). We will "Go from strength to strength, till each appears before God in Zion" (Psalm 84:7). For He says, "In the time of my favor I heard you, and in the day of salvation I helped you. I tell you, now is the time of Gods' favor, now is the day of salvation" (2 Corinthians 6: 2-3).

CHAPTER 27

ONE PLACE I'VE ALWAYS dreamed to work is at United We Stand (UWS). I've had this dream since I was a youth. Many years later, and sometime after I became a believer, I went back to UWS. God called me to go back there to work and serve as an evangelist in the UWS Community. It is a place of mystery to most people. I thank God for this opportunity and for the miraculous way he prepared me to return to UWS for His purposes. My youthful dreams had been fulfilled by the Lord in His way, and not how I had envisioned. I had to be sensitive and careful not to preach my faith aggressively: we need to use wisdom from God. There are many different religions represented at the UWS and you must be very sensitive not to offend anyone there, where world equality is very important. If you push your personal beliefs too much, you risk offending someone and their faith, and you might be removed from your post.

Some extremely intelligent people can often be found working at the UWS Organization. When it comes to worldly knowledge, some of them are bordering on genius. There are ambassadors of various countries and representatives of various international organizations from all over the world; not your average person. Unfortunately, a high IQ can sometimes make it difficult to adopt the humble spirit that is required to come to the Lord. But I know the power of the gospel and I know He will perform miracles, not by my might but by His Holy Spirit. I keep in my mind: "The weapons we fight with are not the weapons of the world. On the contrary, they have divine power to demolish strongholds. We demolish arguments and every pretension that sets itself up against the knowledge of God, and we take captive every thought to make it obedient to Christ" (2 Corinthians 10:4-5). I asked for God's wisdom to be a dignified person in my deeds and to be a good "peace messenger" to act as Jesus taught me: "I am sending you out like sheep among wolves. Therefore, be as shrewd as snakes and as innocent as doves" (Matthew 10:16).

You can share the gospel with the UWS community, but the only thing that can really reach them is the power of the Holy Spirit. "For it is written: "I will destroy the wisdom of the wise; the intelligence of the intelligent I will frustrate" (1 Corinthians 1:19), "so that no one may boast before him" (1 Corinthians 1:29). When people experience trials and challenges, especially in family matters, the Lord opens a door to minister to them. God gave me wisdom to find opportunities to meet with senior scholars, diplomats, officials, and ambassadors. I had the opportunity to share the love of God over lunch, coffee, and during conferences, etc.

One day a large group of directors were discussing an issue. For some time, the directors were arguing and fighting with each other. The mood in the meeting was very heavy and conflicted. One director noticed I was sitting there quietly observing and asked for my opinion. I suggested that all their proposals were good, but that I needed to pray first before I could offer any comments or proposals. The room became very quiet and the meeting was dismissed. A short time later, I received a letter of apology from the group of directors. They were embarrassed by their angry and immature display of behavior. As a Christian, God can use you as a light in this sometimes very dark world. You can be the messenger, if you are a believer of Jesus Christ. Your daily deeds can glorify God's name, often without realizing it.

Many Christians have knowledge of the Bible, but we need to act on God's word too. "Do not merely listen to the word, and so deceive yourselves. Do what it says" (James 1:22). The Lord gave me wisdom at UWS to serve the Lord in each situation He put in front of me. My old friend, who had tremendous wisdom and knowledge, and a former High Official, was not a believer. After about twenty-five years, I accidentally bumped into him in front of the building. I shared the gospel with him, and months later, I could see in his eyes that God's love softened his heart, when I prayed in the hospital for him.

One of my office colleagues told me that the organization has a special chapel. "Really?" I asked surprisingly. One day, after our lunch, she took me there. That day, the Holy Spirit guided me into the small, but beautiful church center. Fortunately, at that time, I found a group of people praying there. I met a sister in Christ, named Wen Shu, who introduced the other members of the small group to me. She told me God brought me to them, to form a team to preach the gospel for UWS. She is one amazing sister with strong faith in the Lord and was baptized in the Holy Spirit and water not that long ago. She asked if I knew where she worked, as she needed some support to glorify the name of Jesus Christ at UWS. I assured her I would support her in whatever way I could.

Wen Shu had been very sick. She works in the President's Office – the most powerful office in this organization. She had very bad health challenges with her kidneys. "I was supposed to be let go" she confided in me. "My sister who lives in Chicago, Illinois asked me to come and meet her pastor the Rev. Duke James, so the pastor could pray for me. I flew there, and her pastor prayed for me.

I was healed instantly. I returned to work and the President couldn't believe his eyes that I was still alive and in good health. Before that, they had planned to fire me due to my poor health. I was unable to handle so many jobs. After returning from that trip healed, Human Resources hired me back. I was supposed to die the next week."

I thought to myself, "Surely it was God's grace and healing power that healed her of this life-threatening illness."

She continued, "Everyone in my department was impacted. My story touched everyone who knew of my illness and heard of my miraculous healing. After this gift, I began to preach the gospel myself in my own office. I have been completely healed, so I shared my testimony with twenty to thirty colleagues and half of them have been baptized." What a fantastic and amazing testimony sister Wen shared with me. How incredible is the power of our Lord Jesus! It was through her pure, simple heart of love for the Lord that she began boldly preaching the gospel at UWS, despite the many high ranked officers there. Her story drew me to fellowship with her in Christ, and to take every possible opportunity to work with her and a few others as a team to "lift up" Jesus' Name. I feel so thankful and blessed that the Holy Spirit led me to Wen Shu and the chapel. "But the Lord said to Ananias, "Go! This man is my chosen instrument to carry my name before the Gentiles and their kings and before the people of Israel. I will show him how much he must suffer for my name" (Acts 9:15).

One day I was invited to the small group to give my testimony and preach the gospel to a group of thirty people. God's Holy Spirit was there working greatly on the hearts of these high official newcomers to the organization. After we prayed and laid hands on them, they were miraculously baptized by the Holy Spirit, and started instantly speaking in tongues. It was incredible. All glory goes to our Lord!

I joined Wen Shu's team of prayer warriors and evangelists. I saw God orchestrating opportunities to minister through her and other sisters in Christ. We share our testimony and try to serve the unbelievers at UWS as each individual situation allows and opportunities arise. Yes, it is a blessing and joy for us to know "there will be more rejoicing in heaven over one sinner who repents..." (Luke 15:7). The Holy Spirit knows this organization needs a Pastor empowered by the Holy Spirit, and sent an anointed pastor from Chicago to fly to Boston to pray for the organization. "The Spirit searches all things, even the deep things of God" (1 Corinthians 2:10).

We pray for the unbelievers to view their lives in the light of God's truth, working for the real King; our Lord Jesus, rather than only working for the rulers of the earth. "For we are God's masterpiece. He has created us anew in Christ Jesus, so we can do the good things he planned for us long ago" (Ephesians 2:10).

We hope and pray their identity is not found in fame, power, or money, but rather in Christ Jesus and that they may have eternal life with God the Father. We believe the Holy Spirit Himself will preach the gospel there to save more of his chosen people from all nations. "In the last days, the mountain of the Lords' temple will be established as chief among the mountains; it will be raised above the hills, and all nations will stream to it. Many peoples will come and say, 'come, let us go up to the mountain of the Lord, to the house of the God of Jacob. He will teach us His ways, so that we may walk in His paths'. The law will go out from Zion, the word of the Lord from Jerusalem. He will judge between the nations and will settle disputes for many peoples" (Isaiah 2:2-4). Like Isaiah the prophet it is also a foundational belief of UWS to keep the world in security, peace, and harmony among all the nations. God's word was calligraphically engraved in a stone wall facing the President's office, "They will beat their swords into plowshares and their spears into pruning hooks. Nation will not take up sword against nation, nor will they train for war anymore" (Isaiah 2:4B). May God bless His word, and may God's peace, love and hope be in all nations for all His people.

For the very first time in UWS's history, the gospel of Jesus Christ was preached in the Chief Congregation by Pastor Brian Williams. He was the first person ever to give his personal testimony of Jesus' gospel in his life, to so many high official participants and world leaders, including the President, and Vice President of the Chief Congregation. According to a data report, this historical moment of Pastor Brian Williams' testimony and his preaching was aired and watched by two billion people worldwide that day. God is moving in UWS's community. The gospel is boldly being preached on this world platform. He is giving us wisdom to proclaim the name of Jesus. "But seek first his kingdom and his righteousness, and all these things will be given to you as well" (Matthew 6:33). May His Kingdom, Holy Spirit, love, and peace rule your heart to share His good news with the world.

The place that used to be my "idol" is now being transformed into a place where I am commissioned to share God's gospel. What a great mission God assigned especially to me. His way is beyond what I can even comprehend and understand myself. Hallelujah! I believe that as your heart is committed to God's Kingdom, He will certainly and graciously give you power. As the Holy Spirit dwells in you, He will put you in a "High" place for His Kingdom at the right time and in the right place. All glory goes to God!

CHAPTER 28

"All this is from God, who reconciled us to himself through Christ and gave us the ministry of reconciliation: that God was reconciling the world to himself in Christ, not counting men's sins against them. And he has committed to us the message of reconciliation. We are therefore Christ's ambassadors, as though God were making his appeal through us. We implore you on Christ's behalf: Be reconciled to God. God made him who had no sin to be sin for us, so that in him we might become the righteousness of God" (2 Corinthians 5:18-21).

WE ARE ALL GOD'S appointed Ambassadors of the gospel for his Kingdom. It has been the greatest honor to serve Him in giving the United We Stand Peace Message. I feel God has called me and commissioned my life to spread the love of our Lord Jesus Christ and the good news and peace of Jesus' gospel in the UWS organization. Whenever I travel, or wherever I go, whether I travel by car or by airplane, official or unofficial business, I try to make good use of my time and share God's word with the people the Lord puts in my path. I am not ashamed of this gospel, because it is the power of God for the salvation of everyone who believes (Romans 1:16).

From a small village to a world stage perched in an international community, I feel an urgency to make Jesus known to all nations, to the best of my ability. This is my way of understanding God's commission to me as an "International Peace Messenger". Mordecai told Esther "And who knows but that you have come to a royal position for such a time as this?" to ask her to request to see the King (Esther 4:14). We should know clearly, that we are being graciously set apart in this world as a chosen people to live for our Lord. "Therefore, show these men the proof of your love and the reason for our pride in you, so that the churches can see it" (2 Corinthians 8:24). "For Christ's love compels us, because we are convinced that one died for all, and therefore all die. And he died for all, that those who live should no longer live for themselves but for him who died for them and was raised again" (2 Corinthians 5:14-15). In all honesty the Lord allows me to spend time sharing the gospel with the most people I meet and get to spend quality time with.

Over many years, I have met many diplomats, mayors, business people, and high-ranking officials from all over the world. I especially share our Lord Jesus with those I meet when I go to China. As a great gift, I usually give them a Bible prior to departure and tell them to take it home for their personal, private reading. I also share the gospel with new friends, Muslims, and Monks. I hand out tracts or flyers about the gospel on the street and at the entrance of super markets in different cities in the U.S. Sometimes I am looked down upon, but my heart is very joyful even when I face "rejection". People may throw away my fliers and humiliate me, but it's okay because I know that to suffer for Jesus' Kingdom is my daily bread and life. It is on the cross that: "Surely he took up our infirmities and carried our sorrows...But he was pierced for our transgressions, he was crushed for our iniquities; the punishment that brought us peace was upon him, and by his wounds we are healed" (Isaiah 53:4-5).

Many times, we participated in overseas missions in different countries to spread the gospel. We were met and received by many devoted brothers and sisters in Christ. Overseas missionary work is as a commandment given by our Lord Jesus to reap the souls all over the world with the power He gives us. "But you will receive power when the Holy Spirit comes upon you, and you will be my witnesses in Jerusalem and in all Judea and Samaria, and to the end of the earth." (Acts 1:8)

I believe your spirit is being plugged into the Holy Spirit while you are reading this, my testimony, and that His great love, compassion, and commission will flow through you to sow more for God's Kingdom and not for the "wicked and adulterous generation" we are now in. Sow nothing and reap nothing. No suffering, no gain, no resurrected life in you, means no eternal life for you. However, it is a certainty that if your life is resurrected today, from now until eternity, you will be with our glorious King Jesus together in His Kingdom. May God's truth be with you and His grace sufficient for you.

> "Grace, mercy and peace from God the Father and from Jesus Christ, the Father's Son, will be with us in truth and love" (2 John:3).

Final Thoughts

I, (Peter Pan Shi) your dear brother and companion in the suffering and kingdom and patient endurance that are ours in Jesus, am with you today because of the word of God and the testimony of Jesus (Revelation 1:9). I am very thankful for your great love, as I share with you my resurrected life of miracles to bring glory to our Lord Jesus.

I, like you, have been chosen "Now get up and stand on your feet. I have appeared to you to appoint you as a servant as and as a witness of what you will see of me" (Acts 26:16).

WORSHIP

Do you worship the Lord in Spirit? Have you been filled up with/by the Holy Spirit in your heart? "when the true worshipers will worship the Father in the Spirit and in truth, for they are the kind of worshipers the Father seeks. God is spirit, and his worshipers must worship in the Spirit and in truth" (John 4:23-24).

While John encourages believers to worship in God's truth and in God's Spirit, it is also good to be in God's word daily. His word is our daily bread. Jesus is called the "Bread of Life" and His words nourish our spiritual lives.

Our sins <u>may</u> block us from feeling God's presence. <u>Sometimes</u> our sins (our dishonesty, our lies, our pride, greediness, un-forgiveness, jealousy, and our unbelief in our Lord's love keep us from seeing the spiritual realm. When I was a young boy and did not know God or that Jesus is God, God showed me a bright flash of light. This was God's favor on me that he revealed this amazing vision to me. After I came to the Lord, and hungered and thirsted to know more of Him, to have more of Him, he continued to reveal Himself to me through visions. I saw my friend's stomach surrounded by bright and beautiful colors, much like a rainbow. I believe God had intended for me to tell her that she would have a baby soon. This friend had been praying to get pregnant for a very long time, and after this vision, she had a baby nine months later. God allowed me to prophesy for my friend. There are times I can also see "dark snakes" flying on somebody's forehead. Perhaps God is revealing to me that the enemy has entered this person, or that I need to be careful about my relationship with this person. Or maybe God is revealing Satan is attacking this person. The more I abide in Jesus, and read His word daily, and the more I meditate on His word, the more visions God gives me. Sometimes I may be resting on the sofa, and I see glorious clouds on the ceiling of my house. I sometimes see clouds floating around the light fixtures at church. The more time I spend with Jesus, the more I love Him and don't want to hurt Him. Our sin not only hurts us and other people, but it hurts God. The closer we get to God, the more we see our sinfulness. I need to abide in God and rest in His Spirit to help deliver me from temptation and overcome my sin. We can't do this in our own strength. Only the Holy Spirit has the power to help us overcome our sin.

We need God's Holy Spirit abiding in us for us to be holy and sanctified, to prevent repeatedly making bad decisions in our lives. "Examine yourselves to see whether you are in the faith; test yourselves" (2 Corinthians 13:5A). We must yield to the Holy Spirit in us and "watch and pray" to have self-control in all aspects of our lives and to obey God's will, living a holy life that glorifies our Lord.

"Make every effort to live in peace with everyone and to be holy; without Holiness no one will see the Lord" (Hebrews 12:14). Jesus chooses us to love us and He said "If you love me, keep my commands. And I will ask the Father, and he will give you another advocate to help you and be with you forever—the Spirit of truth. The world cannot accept him, because it neither sees him nor knows him. But you know him, for he lives with you and will be in you. I will not leave you as orphans; I will come to you" (John 14: 15-18). We have this Holy Spirit as a guaranteed deposit inside of us to receive God's abundant love forever. His Love Never forsakes you!

Our sin keeps us from receiving all the good God has for us. "Submit yourselves, then, to God. Resist the devil, and he will flee from you. Come near to God and he will come near to you. Wash your hands, you sinners and purify your hearts..." (James 4:7-8A). Your spiritual eyes will be opened when you have faith in God's Spirit, Jesus, His truth, and love. The Lord told Moses how he would bless the Israelites; "The LORD bless you and keep you; the LORD make his face shine on you and be gracious to you; the LORD turn his face toward you and give you peace" (Numbers 6:24-26). God is the same today as he was yesterday. We can't have victory or be holy in our own strength. We need Jesus to live a holy and victorious life, and if we love and trust in Jesus, He will help us. What a lovely and amazing promise to live IN Christ rather than in our own flesh and knowledge.

WARNINGS ABOUT OUR ENEMY, THE DEVIL

Our beloved brother John, in his book acknowledges that "We know that we are children of God, and that the whole world is under the control of the evil one" (1 John 5:19).

Peter, in the book of First Peter says, "Be alert and of sober mind. Your enemy the devil prowls around like a roaring lion looking for someone to devour" (1 Peter 5:8).

Jesus clearly states in the book of John "The thief comes only to steal and kill and destroy; I have come that they may have life, and have it to the full" (John 10:10).

Paul again says in Ephesians that "Finally, be strong in the Lord and in his mighty power. Put on the full armor of God so that you can take your stand against the devil's schemes. For our struggle is not against flesh and blood, but against the rulers, against the authorities, against the powers of this dark world and against the spiritual forces of evil in the heavenly realms" (Ephesians 6:10-12).

Thanks be to God, that we as children of God, do not have to do battle ourselves in this corrupt world, but rather take refuge in God and in his mighty power. "For what I received I passed on to you as of first importance: that Christ died for our sins according to the Scriptures, that he was buried, that he was raised on the third day according to the Scriptures, and that he appeared to Cephas, and then to the Twelve. After that, he appeared to more than five hundred of the brothers and sisters at the same time, most of whom are still living, though some have fallen asleep" (1 Corinthians 15:3-6).

Jesus has won the battle of sin and death through his death on the cross and his resurrection from death. Jesus is now sitting at the right hand of God interceding for you and me in heaven. If we trust and love Jesus, we have victory over sin, death, and Satan through Jesus' work on the cross.

Through Jesus' death and resurrection comes the salvation and the power and the kingdom of our Lord, and the authority of Christ.

In Revelation "The great dragon was hurled down—that ancient serpent called the devil, or Satan, who leads the whole world astray. He was hurled to the earth, and his angels with him. Then I heard a loud voice in heaven say: 'Now have come the salvation and the power and the kingdom of our God, and the authority of his Messiah. For the accuser of our brothers, who accuses them before our God day and night, has been hurled down. They triumphed over him by the blood of the Lamb and by the word of their testimony...'" (Revelation 12:9-11).

Sharing His Word

My Lord redeemed me through Christ who died for my sins, "But God demonstrates his own love for us in this: While we were still sinners, Christ died for us" (Romans 5:8). "Therefore, if anyone is in Christ, the new creation has come: The old has gone, the new is here!" (2 Corinthians 5:17). I want to praise his great miraculous name Jesus Christ. "Salvation is found in no one else, for there is no other name under heaven given to mankind by which we must be saved" (Acts 4:12). "Our God is a God who saves; from the Sovereign LORD comes escape from death" (Psalm 68:20). I worship him daily; "Seven times a day I praise you for your righteous laws" (Psalm 119:164).

"Yet, you are enthroned as the Holy One; you are the one Israel praises" (Psalm 22:3). I grow in my daily relationship with Him through praising and worshiping. My attitude is to sing and to dance every day and "Shout for joy to the LORD, all the earth. Worship the LORD with gladness; come before him with joyful songs...enter his gates with thanksgiving and his courts with praise" (Psalm 100:1-4).

I want to preach every day because I have found that when I am weak, if I go out to preach the gospel to strangers on the street, I find all my weakness is suddenly gone. I don't notice when it leaves, but after preaching, I feel joyful and I feel filled with God's power. "For I am not ashamed of the gospel, because it is the power of God that brings salvation to everyone who believes..." (Romans 1: 16). If you want power, try going out to preach the gospel. If you want to be totally released from all your bondage, I encourage you to share God's truth with others. If you want to be healed physically and spiritually, share

God's word and preach the gospel. If you want to be SAVED from your life circumstances, tell someone of the unconditional love and sacrifice of Jesus. Be a great witness for our Lord Jesus who is watching, caring, leading, and protecting you inside and out, day and night. I have been through many trials in my life, and I have found that sharing the gospel has helped me both physically and spiritually. I am certain you will experience God's abundant blessings when you tell others of His great love and power.

It is easier said than done to be a warrior "fighting a good fight for Jesus' Kingdom". However, acting on your faith helps you to experience the power and strength God has given to you. When the Holy Spirit is upon you and the Lords words are inside of you, then you will be fully and wholly empowered to preach the gospel to all nations. Preaching the gospel is the manifestation of God's power upon you and the filling up with God's word and abiding in Jesus' Holy Spirit. Just as scripture says:

"The Spirit of the Sovereign LORD is on me, because the LORD has anointed me to proclaim good news to the poor. He has sent me to bind up the brokenhearted, to proclaim freedom for the captives and release from darkness for the prisoners, to proclaim the year of the LORD's favor" (Isaiah 61:1-2A).

I want to "Sing to the Lord, praise his name; proclaim his salvation day after day. Declare his glory among the nations, his marvelous deeds among all peoples" (Psalm 96:2-3).

I encourage you to share your great testimony of God's power, grace, and work in your life. I strongly desire to make this testimony of Jesus, my personal story, available by and through the help of the Holy Spirit to you as my sincere thanks for all the Lord has done for me. I believe you also have an amazing and personal story and witness to Jesus, to share with the world and bring glory to the Lord Jesus Christ.

His life of resurrection will be manifested through you as you become a light to your neighbors. We are born to live out our vibrant life, godly purpose, faith, and relationships in patience, harmony, sacrificial love, hope and endurance despite all persecution and suffering in our circumstances. Through this, we will bless others, and bless our Lord Christ and be blessed and rewarded in God's Kingdom.

Unique in God

Your life is so valued and treasured in this world. You are a most unique and beautiful creation to Him and He desires for you to live for Him in this world. He desires you to glorify His name as His Special Envoy and Ambassador on this earth with His special purpose for you. You are the work of His hands commissioned to shine His light in this dark world. You, and I are designed to bring Him glory. "…everyone who is called by my name, whom I created for my glory, whom I formed and made" (Isaiah 43:7).

In this enormous and mysterious world, do you know that you are a most valued, uniquely designed creature to our God? We are all created by Him in His image. I do not think you can acknowledge this unbelievable and amazing gracious fact until you really know Him in the Lord's Spirit. Psalm 17:8 tells us we are the apple of His eye. He loves you so much, like no one else in this world can. No matter who you are: big or small, young, or old, tall, or short, fat, or skinny, male, or female, poor or rich, believer of Christ or not a believer in Him yet, as long as you are a human being, you are perfectly unique and most beautiful in His eyes, because he created you. He desires for you to seek Him and know Him intimately. God created you, so you are the most blessed creature on this earth and in the whole universe. When you love, trust, and follow Jesus, you become a daughter or son of the King. "But you are a chosen people, a royal priesthood, a holy nation, God's special possession, that you may declare the praises of him who called you out of the darkness into his wonderful light" (1 Peter 2:9). He desires you to respond to Him as he lovingly pursues you the moment you are born, and loved you before you were born. "Before I formed you in the womb I knew you, before you were born I set you apart..." (Jeremiah 1:5A). As a Christian, you know:

"'For in him we live and move and have our being.' As some of your own poets have said, 'We are his offspring'" (Acts 17:28).

"Therefore, since we have been justified through faith, we have peace with God through our Lord Jesus Christ, through whom we have gained access by faith into this grace in which we now stand. And we boast in the hope of the glory of God" (Romans 5:1-2).

"Out of his fullness we have received grace in place of grace already given" (John 1:16).

His Love is IMMEASURABLE.

"For God so loved the world, that he gave His one and only Son, that whoever believes in him should not perish but have eternal life" (John 3:16). God sent his Son, Jesus, to die for you personally. He did not wait for us to stop sinning and become Holy, because we can't in our own strength. He loves you so much, that He gave up His Son for you, so that if you chose to repent, your sins would be paid for. He offers us a plan of salvation. If we choose to follow Christ, He takes your sins and puts them on His Son, Jesus, and credits you with His righteousness, and His goodness. And through Jesus death on the cross and resurrection, if we choose to follow Jesus, we are forgiven of all our sins, past, present, and future sins, and are given eternal life with God forever. This gift is completely free for us to take, but it cost Jesus everything.

He unconditionally loves you and never forsakes you, and he knows every detail of your life:

"And even the very hairs of your head are all numbered" (Matthew 10:30). How marvelous is that? Can you imagine that? He surrounds you from above, from the front and the from the back: "You hem me in behind and before, and you lay your hand upon me. Such knowledge is too wonderful for me, too lofty for me to attain" (Psalm 139:5-6).

He also specially engraved your name in the palm of His hand. "Can a mother forget the baby at her breast and have no compassion on the child she has borne? Though she may forget, I will not forget you! See, I have engraved you on the palms of my hands..." (Isaiah 49:15-16A).

He washes away all our sins without recording or "memorizing" them. "Since you are precious and honored in my sight, and because I love you.." (Isaiah 43:4A). Although you may not see him with your physical eyes, He and His love are real than anything in this world. "But God demonstrates his own love for us in this: While we were still sinners, Christ died for us" (Romans 5:8). "But because of his great love for us, God, who is rich in mercy, made us alive with Christ even when we were dead in transgressions—it is by grace you have been saved. And God raised us up with Christ and seated us with him in the heavenly realms in Christ Jesus, in order that in the coming ages he might show the incomparable riches of his grace, expressed in his kindness to us in Christ Jesus" (Ephesians 2:4-7).

Isn't it wonderful to be thankful to Him all the time? His love is our life. We will perish without His daily love pouring out on us. "The Lord appeared to us in the past, saying: 'I have loved you with an everlasting love; I have drawn you with unfailing kindness'" (Jeremiah 31:3). Do you know and understand his agape love for you? "I pray that out of his glorious riches he may strengthen you with power through his Spirit in your inner being, so that Christ may dwell in your hearts through faith. And I pray that you, being rooted and established in love, may have power together with all the Lord's holy people, to grasp how wide and long and high and deep is the love of Christ, and to know this love that surpasses knowledge--that you may be filled to the measure with all the fullness of God" (Ephesians 3:16-19). Without a doubt, "God is love." "This is how God showed his love among us: He sent his one and only Son into the world that we might live through him. This is love: not that we loved God, but that he loved us and sent his Son as an atoning sacrifice for our sins" (1 John 4:9-10). "And so, we know and rely on the love God has for us. God is love. Whoever lives in love lives in God, and God in them" (1 John 4:16). "We love because he first loved us" (1 John 4:19).

God chose his only Son, Jesus Christ — "A voice came from the cloud saying, 'This is my Son, whom I have chosen; listen to him'" (Luke 9:35). The Lord, Jesus Christ, died on the cross to forgive and to cleanse our sins, making it possible for us to enter his eternal, glorified, blessed, and holy Kingdom. Your believing in Him makes Him pour out His richest love on you because He has chosen you. "For he chose us in him before the creation of the world to be holy and blameless in his sight" (Ephesians 1:4). "Who have been chosen according to the foreknowledge of God the Father, through the sanctifying work of the Spirit, to be obedient to Jesus Christ and sprinkled with his blood: Grace and peace be yours in abundance" (1 Peter 1:2). "But you are a chosen people, a royal priesthood, a holy nation, God's special possession, that you may declare the praises of him who called you out of darkness into his wonderful light" (1 Peter 2:9). His love chooses you, just as He chose Jacob, His servant of Israel. The Bible says:

"For the sake of Jacob my servant, of Israel my chosen, I summon you by name and bestow on you a title of honor, though you do not acknowledge me. I am the Lord and there is no other; apart from me there is no God. I will strengthen you, though you do not acknowledge me, so that from the rising of the sun to the place of its setting people may know there is none besides me. I am the Lord, and there is no other. I form the light and create darkness, I bring prosperity and create disaster; I, the LORD, do all these things" (Isaiah 45:4-7).

He loves to choose you for an unchangeable promise prepared for you. "I will go before you and will level the mountains; I will break down gates of bronze and cut through bars of iron. I will give you hidden treasures, riches stored in secret places, so that you may know that I am the LORD, the God of Israel, who summons you by name" (Isaiah 45: 2-3).

"He Loves you to Choose you, and He Chooses you to Love you!" --- this is my word from God for you my dear fellow brothers and sisters. I pray for you that His richest love is upon you today to renew your heart and spirit for an abundant life ahead of you. I pray for God's abundance in your family, in your work and in strengthening you and giving you good health. No matter what circumstance you are in, remember one thing, He is faithful, just, merciful and kind. Have faith in Him and be courageous in His word and Spirit that He has placed before you. "He has placed before you an open door that no one can shut for you" (Revelation 3:8). "Now to him who is able to do immeasurably more than all we ask or imagine, according to his power that is at work within us, to him be glory in the church and in Christ Jesus throughout all generations, for ever and ever! Amen" (Ephesians 3:20).

Essential Truths for Your Questions and Concerns:

1. What does it mean to be a Christian?

To be a Christian means you are now a child of God. "Yet to all who did receive him, to those who believed in his name, he gave the right to become children of God" (John 1:12). To be a Christian means your life is in Christ, not of this world. You have repented of your sins, and are forgiven of them. You have crossed over from Spiritual death to life as you have sincerely prayed for Jesus to come to live inside you, trusting in the power of His shed blood on the cross to cleanse you of your sins. You now have victory over sin, death, guilt, and Satan through the work of Jesus death on the cross and resurrection. You receive power from the Holy Spirit which helps you overcome sin. Sin no longer has power over you. The Holy Spirit is a gift from Jesus to you and will give you wisdom, help, comfort, and power through your yielding to the Holy Spirit who dwells in you. You are still with sin, but now you stand in Jesus' righteousness. You are no longer a slave to sin, but are powerful in Christ Jesus. "In the same way, count yourselves dead to sin and alive to God in Christ Jesus" (Romans 6:11).

You are separated and chosen by the Lord to live for God as a living sacrifice and to glorify Jesus Christ in all aspects of your life. "Then Jesus said to his disciples, 'Whoever wants to be my disciple must deny themselves and take up their cross and follow me. For whoever wants to save their life will lose it, but whoever loses their life for me will find it'" (Matthew 16:24-25). You are now considered one of the "Chosen" ones. You are now considered righteous in Christ Jesus. "Surely, LORD, you bless the righteous; you surround them with your favor as with a shield" (Psalm 5:12). As a Christian, you are protected and blessed by God. Psalm 91 says "He who dwells in the shelter of the Most High will rest in the shadow of the almighty. I will say of the Lord, 'He is my refuge and my fortress, my God, in whom I trust.'"

You are now able to receive all of God's promises he makes to His children. There are many wonderful and beautiful promises God makes to his children in the Bible. One promise He makes to us is "The LORD will fight for you; you need only to be still" (Exodus 14:14). "He gives strength to the weary and increases the power of the weak" (Isaiah 40:29). "...but those who hope in the LORD will renew their strength. They will soar on wings like eagles; they will run and not grow weary, they will walk and not be faint" (Isaiah 40:31). "So, do not fear, for I am with you; do not be dismayed, for I am your God. I will strengthen you and help you; I will uphold you with my righteous right hand" (Isaiah 41:10). "...no weapon forged against you will prevail, and you will refute every tongue that accuses you. This is the heritage of the servants of the LORD, and this is their vindication from me," declares the LORD'" (Isaiah 54:17). "If any of you lacks wisdom, you should ask God, who gives generously to all without finding fault, and it will be given to you" (James 1:5). "Submit yourselves, then, to God. Resist the devil, and he will flee from you" (James 4:7). "'For I know the plans I have for you', declares the LORD, 'plans to prosper you and not to harm you, plans to give you hope and a future'" (Jeremiah 29:11). There are numerous promises God has for you, now that you are His. I encourage you to read the Bible and find each special promise He has made to you. Claim and receive these promises.

"Dear friends, now we are children of God, and what we will be has not yet been made know. But we know that when Christ appears, we shall be like him, for we shall see him as he is. All

116

who have this hope in him purify themselves, just as he is pure" (1 John 3:2-3). One day when Christ returns, you will be perfect just as he is perfect.

2. **How can I become a Christian?**

    There are no special requirements for you to become a child of God. Confess your sins and ask Jesus to forgive you. Ask in prayer for Jesus to come into your life. "Ask and it will be given to you; seek and you will find; knock and the door will be opened for you" (Matthew 7:7). Show your belief in Jesus' life, death, and resurrection with action TODAY by confessing with your mouth that Jesus is your Lord and believing in your heart that God forgave all your sins through Jesus' shed blood on the cross. "For it is with your heart that you believe and are justified, and it is with your mouth that you profess your faith and are saved" (Romans 10:10).

3. **How can I be 100% assured of being saved for eternal life with Jesus?**

    If I confess my sins and I trust and believe that Jesus is God, who died on the cross for me and was resurrected from death, and I surrender my life to Jesus, I have eternal life with Jesus. "Jesus answered, 'I am the way and the truth and the life. No one comes to the Father except through me'" (John 14:6).

4. **How can I be assured of receiving eternal life with God now and that I will enter the radiant and glorious Kingdom of God with Jesus in the future?**

    My spirit is made alive in Christ. All who believe Jesus is God and who place their faith in Him are His children and can trust that the Lord Jesus, has specially saved a place in Heaven for us as He promised. "And if I go and prepare a place for you, I will come back and take you to be with me that you also may be where I am" (John 14:3). "The Spirit himself testifies with our spirit that we are God's children" (Romans 8:16). God's children can know that they have eternal life with Jesus. "Now it is God who makes both us and you stand firm in Christ. He anointed us, set his seal of ownership on us, and put his Spirit in our hearts as a deposit, guaranteeing what is to come" (2 Corinthians 1:21-22).

If you humbly confess your sins, and trust and love Jesus as the God Almighty, your heart is justified in believing Jesus is your personal Lord and you are saved. The grace of salvation and truth came through Jesus. "As for you, you were dead in your transgressions and sins, in which you used to live when you followed the ways of this world and of the ruler of the kingdom of the air, the spirit who is now at work in those who are disobedient. All of us also lived among them at one time, gratifying the cravings of our flesh and following its desires and thoughts. Like the rest, we were by nature deserving of wrath. But because of His great love for us, God, who is rich in mercy, made us alive with Christ even when we were dead in transgressions – it is by grace you have been saved. And God raised us up with Christ and seated us with him in the heavenly realms in Christ Jesus, in order that in the coming ages he might show the incomparable riches of his grace, expressed in his kindness to us in Christ Jesus. For it is by grace you have been saved, through faith—and this is not from yourselves, it is the gift of God--not by works, so that no one can boast" (Ephesians 2:1-9).

5. **Did God really forgive and forget all my sins and transgressions?**
    Yes, He surely did. "I have swept away your offenses like a cloud, your sins like the morning mist. Return to me, for I have redeemed you" (Isaiah 44:22). "Forgetting what is behind and straining toward what is ahead" (Philippians 3:13B). "For I will forgive their wickedness and will remember their sins no more" (Jeremiah 31:34B).

6. **If I am a Christian will I have a new heart and a new spirit in me?**
    Yes, after salvation you have a new life in Christ with a new spirit because Jesus's spirit is in your heart. "We were therefore buried with him though baptism into death in order that, just as Christ was raised from the dead through the glory of the Father, we too

may live a new life" (Romans 6:4). "You however, are not in the realm of the flesh but are in the realm of the Spirit, if indeed the Spirit of God lives in you. And if anyone does not have the Spirit of Christ, they do not belong to Christ" (Romans 8:9). "Therefore, if anyone is in Christ, the new creation has come; the old has gone, the new is here" (2 Corinthians 5:17). You are holy, set apart from the world.

7.   **Do I need to be water baptized?**

As an act of obedience, if you want to proclaim and declare your love for Jesus to the world, it is an amazing experience to be baptized in water. You can be baptized in a church baptismal tank, in the ocean, or in any body of water, or sprinkled with water (under special circumstance). You can be baptized by a pastor, deacon, or a brother or sister in Christ. Jesus calls us to make disciples of all nations baptizing them in the name of the Father, the Son and the Holy Spirit. Baptism in water is like John's baptism, for repentance. Baptism in the Holy Spirit with fire is only possible through the Lord Jesus Christ. 'I baptize you with water for repentance. But after me comes one who is more powerful than I, whose sandals I am not worthy to carry. He will baptize you with the Holy Spirit and fire" (Matthew 3:11). There is a physical, public baptism in water and a personal, intimate one in the Holy Spirit. Ephesians 4:5 says "One Lord, one faith, one baptism;". However, the thief on the cross didn't have time to be baptized in water, yet he received eternal life with Jesus and God, because he acknowledged Jesus to be the Messiah and devoted what was left of his life to Jesus.

8.   **Do I have to go to church to worship God?**

God desires us to worship and praise our Lord in His Spirit in His House. "But I, by your great mercy, will come into your house; in reverence will I bow down toward your holy temple" (Psalm 5:7). "Praise the LORD. Praise the name of the LORD; praise Him, you servants of the LORD, you who minister in the house of the LORD in the courts of the house of our God" (Psalm 135:1-2). "And let us consider how we may spur one another on toward love and good deeds, not giving up meeting together, as some are in the habit of doing..." (Hebrews 10:24-25A).

9. **Is it ok to worship God at home by myself, without ever having to go to Church on Sunday?**

No, you should go to Church together with your brothers and sisters in Christ, as One Body of Christ to praise and worship our Lord Jesus Christ. In Jesus, we are one big family in Jesus' blood and one body in His Spirit. "For we are all baptized by one Spirit into one body..." (1 Corinthians 12:13), and Jesus "will not leave you as orphans" feeling lonely there by yourself (John 14:18). It is good to meet with other believers to worship God together as one family of believers. At church, you may also connect with other believers you can relate to, pray with, and pray for. Sometimes when we go through trials, we need to surrender them to God to help us through the difficult circumstances. However, it is also helpful in the storms of our lives to share our burdens with other believers who can come alongside us and pray with us. "Though one may be overpowered, two can defend themselves. A cord of three strands is not quickly broken" (Ecclesiastes 4:12).

10. **Why is it important to go to church on Sunday?**

Sometimes it might be difficult or challenging to want to attend church. If you find that the case, go anyway, and pray that the Lord will give you an open and soft heart to receive His word for you. The enemy who rules this world, doesn't want us to go to church and hear God's word for us. He wants to distract us from going to church, reading the Bible, worshiping God, praising Jesus, receiving healing, serving others, and learning more about God. It is a spiritual battle. However, we can depend and trust in God to fight these spiritual battles for us. We need only to be still and know that He is God. Life has many troubles, but we can overcome our circumstances with God's help and power. Going to church, hearing God's word and fellowshipping with other believers can help us stay grounded in Christ. The word of God nourishes us spiritually, it comforts us, heals us, and gives us wisdom and strength.

Your heart should always be longing for God and you should always set your eyes, heart and mind upon the Lord - not upon any other. Don't set your eyes on your own "god or idol" like people, things, fame, title, or anything that distracts your attention away from Jesus. "Praise the Lord, Praise God in his sanctuary; praise him in his mighty heavens" (Psalm 150: 1). Come to His sanctuary with a fearful and joyful heart. "Guard your steps when you go to the house of God. Go near to listen rather than to offer the sacrifice of fools, who do not know that they do wrong" (Ecclesiastes 5:1).

11. **Why should I listen to and obey the teachings of Pastors and Bishops?**

In general, you should listen and obey the sermons of your Pastors or Bishops, as long as they are teaching truths from the Bible. If the teachings are not truths from the Bible, you may reserve the right to reject it and ask the pastor to give the Biblical references to support his sermon. "All Scripture is God-breathed and is useful for teaching, rebuking, correcting, and training in righteousness, so that the servant of God may be thoroughly equipped for every good work" (2 Timothy 3:16-17).

12. **Do I have to physically come to Church to attend services?**

Yes, do your utmost to go to Church in person to worship God and fellowship with others together as One Body in Christ. If for any reason, you are physically unable to attend your Church, I encourage you listen to the sermon online. I have a good friend who has missed a church service and listened to it on-line before, but she said the experience is much richer in person. There is nothing like worshiping the Lord with a family of believers who love and praise Him in song with joy.

13. **What is a tithe?**

A tithe, this monetary offering (money) is God's most blessed covenant for His children. You should keep this covenant for a life-time blessing and practice it, giving ten percent (a tithe literally means one tenth) of your whole income, as a way to worship our Lord. "Bring the whole tithe into the storehouse, that there may be food in my house. 'Test me in this', says the LORD Almighty, 'and see if I will not throw open the floodgates of heaven and pour out so much blessing that there will not be room enough to store it'" (Malachi 3:10). "On the first day of every week, each one of you should set aside a sum of money in keeping with your income, saving it up so that when I come no collections will have to be made" (1 Corinthians 16:2). "Remember this: Whoever sows sparingly will also reap sparingly, and whoever sows generously will also reap generously. Each of you should give what you have decided in your heart to give, not reluctantly or under compulsion, for God loves a cheerful giver. And God is able to bless you abundantly, so that in all things at all times, having all that you need, you will abound in every good work" (2 Corinthians 9:6-8). He will bless you immensely for your faithfulness. You can't out-give God.

Our God is very merciful and kind. The Lord who sees and searches people's hearts for those who are committed to Him and willing to give and sacrifice their treasure for His sake and honor, will open the flood gates to pour His blessings on them. You may also honor the Lord in other ways through your services to Him with the time, gifts and the talents God gives you, and by loving your neighbors.

14. **May I commit sinful actions after being saved? And what happens when I continue to willfully sin after being saved?**
No, you should absolutely not purposefully sin anymore. "In this way we can count ourselves dead to sin but alive to God in Christ Jesus" (Romans 6:11). Once we are saved, and we believe and trust in Jesus, we are united to Jesus in his death for our sins. We die to sin. This means sin no longer has power over our lives. Before we trusted and loved Jesus, sin controlled our lives. Now as believers, we are united to Jesus in His resurrection from death. Our old sinful nature is buried with Jesus, and we are resurrected into a new life in Christ Jesus. We are given a new life and live under God's grace and stand in the righteousness of

Jesus. We now have the power through Jesus to overcome our sin. I encourage you to claim this power and walk in it.

Our God is a merciful, kind and a gracious God. He wants His Children to be as Holy as He is, and He hates all kind of sinful thoughts and actions. Do not let your sins "entangle" your heart. If you commit sin carelessly, and ask for forgiveness, He is faithful to forgive. But if you continuously and consciously act on your sinful desires without end, you should examine yourself and question whether your commitment to God is sincere or if you merely prayed a prayer as "fire insurance". "If we deliberately keep on sinning after we have received the knowledge of the truth, no sacrifice for sins is left, but only a fearful expectation of judgment and of raging fire that will consume the enemies of God" (Hebrews 10:26-27). Jesus answered Peter on how many times to forgive our brother, seven times? His answer was seventy times seven, in other words, keep on forgiving. God is no less forgiving than he expects us to be. He asks that we confess our sins and repent, and we should never abuse His grace or take His sacrifice for granted but His sacrifice covers all our sins, past present and future. Our salvation depends not on our ability not to sin, but on His ability to forgive.

15. **I sometimes continue to sin, as a Christian, does this mean I won't be able to go to heaven?**

Once you are saved, you are always saved. We no longer live in our old sin nature, where sin once had control over us. Once we believe and trust Jesus, the Holy Spirit enters us, and we have power over sin. If we yield to the Holy Spirit in us, we can overcome our sin and say no to sin. As humans, we will still sin, however, sin will not have power over us any longer. Like David who committed sin and cried to God for forgiveness, your repentance is vital and timely because sin has consequences. Just look at David's life. Even though God restored him, the consequences of his sins followed him long afterwards. Remember, salvation had a great price paid by our Lord Jesus and you do not want to take sin lightly. It doesn't just affect you, it affects your relationship and your walk with God and it hurts those you love as well. Surrender every area of your life to Jesus and live in the power of His Holy Spirit in you to help you to run from temptation and say no to sin.

16. **How can I prevent myself from falling or doing sinful things as a new Christian?**
You should live daily in Christ calling for the Holy Spirit of Our Lord to empower you with respect to daily praising, praying, repenting, and forgiving others. Ask the Holy Spirit to help you share the gospel, love your neighbors, to dig into and act on God's word. As we seek to know Jesus better, the Holy Spirit renews our minds. The closer we get to Jesus, the more time we spend with Him, the more our hearts break for what breaks His heart. When we sin, we not only hurt ourselves, and the people around us, but we also hurt God. The more we love and know God, the less we want to hurt Him by acting on our sinful desires. Our actions, words, and thoughts flow out of the love we have in our hearts for Jesus. The closer we get to Jesus, the more we look at ourselves and others around us through His eyes. As we learn more about God through reading His word in the Bible, we learn to love others better. We learn to love ourselves and others as He loves us and others. It is through yielding to the Holy Spirit that lives in us that helps us live a Godly life with a fearful heart to Him, and obey all His commands. "But godliness with contentment is great gain" (1 Timothy 6:6).

17. **Why do some pastors' lives not match their teaching and preaching?** It depends what pastor and what teaching you are talking about. As an anointed pastor, one should obey all God's teaching and apply all the Biblical truths to his life. But unfortunately, sometimes, some pastors don't live according to what they preach. This just shows us that we are all sinners and need Jesus to save us from our sins. Just as Jesus answered the rich young man. "There is no one righteous, not even one; there is no one who understands; there is no one who seeks God. All have turned away they have together become worthless; there is no one who does good, not even one" (Romans 3:10-12) "For all have

sinned and fall short of the glory of God" (Romans 3:23). We do not need to pay so much attention to what his "short comings" are but rather to his correct teachings from the Lord. Having said that, if a pastor is teaching something false or unbiblical, it is our duty as brothers and sisters in Christ to gently restore him. (Galatians 6:1) (Matthew 18:15-17)

18. **My pastors, bishops, deacons, elders, or church members have become my "idol", as I admire them so much.** It is very sinful to love anyone or anything more than God. This is one of the biggest sins against God. In addition, you also do harm to your "idol" as well. In God's eyes, "I am the Lord your God, who brought you out of Egypt (the world), out of the land of slavery. You shall have no other gods before me" (Exodus 20:2-3). In the New Testament, Jesus gave us the greatest commandment when He said: "Love the Lord your God with all your heart and with all your soul and with all your mind." This is the first and greatest commandment. And the second is like it: 'Love your neighbor as yourself'" (Matthew 22:37-39). In Acts 14 When Paul and Barnabas preached in Lystra and Derbe, after Paul healed a lame man who could then stand up on his feet and begin to walk, both Paul and Barnabas were treated like "gods" by the local people. All men wanted to offer sacrifices to them as their gods. "But when the apostles Paul and Barnabas heard of this, they tore their clothes and rushed out into the crowd, shouting: 'Friends, why are you doing this? We too are only human, like you. We are bringing you good news, telling you to turn from these worthless things to the living God, who made heavens and earth and sea and everything in them'" (Acts 14 :14-15). They too let the crowd know it was God who performed the miracles and not themselves. Both as a Christian and as a pastor, we must be very careful not to take credit for God's power in and through us. "So then, no more boasting about men!" (1 Corinthians 2:21B).

19. **What are the greatest benefits of the Christian life?**
As Christians, we have the privilege of knowing the creator of the universe and we can look forward to spending eternity getting to

know Him better, but until that day comes we continue to grow in the fruits of the Spirit as our Lord daily sanctifies us (making us increasingly like Him). We are now considered children of God and all of God's promises in the Bible are meant for us. We are promised God's protection, faithful provision, comfort, healing, wisdom, joy, peace that surpasses all understanding, unlimited love, help, strength, limitless power, deliverance from troubles, abounding grace, His friendship, and the list goes on. One can write books about the benefits of being a Christian.

20. **May I immediately be baptized in water and by the Holy Spirit after I start attending church?**

It is good to be baptized if your motivation, your heart, and your spirit is right and true. "If you declare with your mouth, 'Jesus is Lord', and believe in your heart that God raised him from the dead, you will be saved" (Romans 10:9). Baptism is a gift of grace from God to you "…and no one can say, 'Jesus is Lord,' except by the Holy Spirit" (1 Corinthians 12:3B).

21. **When is the right time to be baptized?**

There is not a fixed time for baptism and everyone's situation is different. If you know and understand the truth about baptism, then you should go for it. Ask about getting water baptized at your church, if the Holy Spirit has put it on your heart. The Church needs to have "water" and the "word of truth". Pastors usually conduct the ceremony, but someone you love (parent, sibling, friend etc.) can also be in the baptismal tank with you. It is the most wonderful experience and testimony to show the world you have decided to love and follow Jesus with your heart and life. It also encourages other believers and non-believers when they see how God is working to transform lives and hearts from death to life. It is a time for great celebration and the Lord is exalted when believers publicly declare their love and devotion to Him.

We can see the story of Philip and the Ethiopian eunuch. This eunuch was reading in the book of Isaiah but did not understand the scripture verse. "Then Philip began with that very passage of Scripture and told him the good news about Jesus. As they traveled along the road, they came to some water and the eunuch said, 'Look, here is water. What can stand in the way of my being baptized?' And he gave orders to stop the chariot. Then both Philip and the eunuch went down into the water and Philip baptized him. When they came up out of the water, the Spirit of the Lord suddenly took Philip away, and the eunuch did not see him again, but went on his way rejoicing" (Acts 8:35-39).

22. **Should I go to a Bible study or Sunday school at church?**

Yes, you should, and I encourage you to do that for spiritual growth. "Let the message of Christ dwell among you richly..." (Colossians 3:16A). "And this is my prayer: that your love may abound more and more in knowledge and depth of insight, so that you may be able to discern what is best and may be pure and blameless for the day of Christ, filled with the fruit of righteousness that comes through Jesus Christ-to the glory and praise of God" (Philippians 1:9). "Whatever happens, conduct yourselves in a manner worthy of the gospel of Christ. Then, whether I come and see you or only hear about you in my absence, I will know that you stand firm in the one Spirit, striving together as one for the faith of the gospel without being frightened in any way by those who oppose you" (Philippians 1:27-28). In the Church, love each other and let everyone see your progress in the truth of our Lord and that your life is in Christ.

23. **As a Christian, should I pray, worship, and read the Bible, daily?**

Absolutely, your spiritual life must be rooted in God's truth, praying in the Holy Spirit. If you speak in tongues, practice speaking in tongues. Apply God's word to your life, by loving your neighbors daily. Make it a habit to read God's word, praying for God's best for you and worshipping Him in truth and spirit. Walk humbly with the Lord in truth. The more you read the Bible, the more you desire to read it and know Him better. The more time we spend with God and in Jesus, the less time we spend "of the world". Our lives, hearts and minds are transformed through the power of the Holy Spirit in us, through God who is revealed to us in the Bible and as we seek Him and talk to Him genuinely and honestly in private.

24. **When should I start serving the Lord?**

You may start serving the Lord as soon as you receive Jesus as your Lord and Savior. However, if you are not yet serving the Lord, I encourage you to start right away. As a child of God, there are many opportunities for you to serve the Lord to your ability. To serve the Lord is a blessing and you can start with the things you least like to do or you can serve Him in the areas of your passion. "Not so with you. Instead, whoever wants to become great among you must be your servant, and whoever wants to be first must be slave of all. For even the Son of Man did not come to be served, but to serve, and to give His life as a ransom for many" (Mark 10:43-45). Whatever or however you choose to serve the Lord, remember your talents, gifts and skills were given to you by the Lord.

25. **Should I join a cell group or small group?**

Yes, it is so great and beneficial to find a cell group or small group and to join with fellow believers who love praising, worshiping, and studying God's word. It is an amazing opportunity to share your new life as a witness for Jesus. More importantly, you can abide in the love of church members, in Biblical truths and strengthen your faith to improve every aspect of your life. In general, a lot of miracles may take place in your cell group as the former disciples found. "They devoted themselves to the apostles' teaching and to the fellowship, to the breaking of bread and to prayer. Everyone was filled with awe, and many wonders and signs performed by the apostles. All the believers were together and had everything in common... Every day they continued to meet together in the temple courts. They broke bread in their homes and ate together with glad and sincere hearts, praising God and enjoying the favor of all the people. And the Lord added to their number daily those who were being saved" (Acts 2:42-47).

26. **Do I need to have a degree from a seminary school to qualify me to serve the Lord?**

No, you are not required to have a degree to serve the Lord. You can start to serve right now, wherever you are. God will use you just as you are and in the process of serving Him and others. "I will give you a new heart and put a new spirit in you; I will remove from you your heart of stone and give you a heart of flesh" (Ezekiel 36:26). "But be sure to fear the Lord and serve Him faithfully with all your heart" (1 Samuel 12:24A); and "To obey is better than sacrifice, and to heed is better that the fat of rams" (1 Samuel 15:22). You will be extremely blessed, and the Lord is exalted, when you serve God at home, at church, in your neighborhood, at work, and at school.

27. **Should I pray before each meal?**

Yes, The Lord desires us to draw close to Him in prayer. It is good to pray before everything, including eating. We may ask the Lord to bless our meal to nourish our bodies, and He will. He desires for us to bring and submit everything to Him in prayer. He desires to bless us as we draw close to Him in daily prayer and seek Him daily. Prayer before meals will not only benefit us to nourish our physical body, but will also nourish us in mind and spirit. Thus, pray, bless, and give thanks with gladness like the disciples in Acts, to enjoy the food God daily provides us. It is good to thank God for everything He gives us. The Lord is glorified when we have a continuous "attitude of gratitude" towards God and His many gifts and blessings. We draw near to the Lord in our thankfulness for all that He is and all that He does for us.

It is also important to pray before making big decisions. Bring every situation to the Lord and ask for wisdom and He will give it to you. Pray for your spouse, children, family, friends, and neighbors. Pray for the leaders of every nation. Whatever you are doing or involved with, bring it to the Lord to bless, direct and guide. He is the maker of the universe, He has the best plans, directions and is the best help available.

28. As a Christian, may I drink liquor or wine? May I smoke?

Our body is God's temple and we must take care of it according to God's will, making it stronger and stronger to live for Jesus on the earth as a "shining light" in this dark world. Your physical body is also important to glorify God's name in your daily life. "Don't you know that you yourselves are God's temple and that God's Spirit dwells in your midst? If anyone destroys Gods temple, God will destroy that person; for God's temple is sacred, and you are that temple" (1 Corinthians 3:16-17). If drinking a little wine or liquor is doing good to your health, you are okay to drink it. Just like Paul taught Timothy to "Stop drinking only water, and use a little wine because of your stomach and your frequent illnesses" (1 Timothy 5:23). However, "Do not get drunk on wine, which leads to debauchery. Instead be filled with the Spirit, speaking to one another with psalms, hymns, and songs from the Spirit. Sing and make music from your heart to the Lord, always giving thanks to God the Father for everything, in the name of our Lord Jesus Christ" (Ephesians 5:18). "Wine is a mocker and beer a brawler; whoever is led astray by them is not wise" (Proverbs 20:1). Smoking is prohibited in public everywhere in today's society and proved harmful to your health. Stop it immediately, and if you have no strength to quit, I suggest you come to Church to be baptized, be filled by the Holy Spirit, so that you may better understand the Lord's will for you. Our Lord is the best doctor who can heal every kind of disease and addiction.

29. Do I need to fast? What does fasting mean? How long do I need to fast? Will my faith get stronger if I fast?

In fasting, your purpose is to be more intimate in your relationship with our Lord, while you pray in spirit and truth searching for God's will to sanctify your life before God. Never try to use fasting as a tool or for your own purposes to "profit goodness" out of it, or your fasting is not acceptable to the Lord. Fast as you feel the Lord is calling you to fast.

The Lord said: "Is it not this the kind of fasting I have chosen: to loose the chains of injustice and untie the cords of the yoke, to set the oppressed free and break every yoke? Is it not to share your food with the hungry and to provide the poor wanderer with shelter - when you see him naked, to clothe them, and not to turn away from your own flesh and blood?" (Isaiah 58: 6-7). This is the kind of fasting God requires from us.

30. **I can't fast since my body doesn't allow me to fast? Will my faith get weaker if I do not fast?**

If your body does not allow you to endure fasting, do not fast. God doesn't ask you to do anything he doesn't equip you to do. Your faith depends on God's word and His spirit moving inside you, so do not worry if you are not able to fast.

31. **I am still unable to get free or delivered from my habitual sin after fasting and praying. How can I be delivered from my habitual sin?**

Battling sin in your own flesh is difficult. You need to ask the Holy Spirit to come into your heart: "If we confess our sins, he is faithful and just and will forgive us our sins and purify us from all unrighteousness" (1 John 1:9). As Paul said: "What a wretched man I am! Who will rescue me from this body that is subject to death? Thanks be to God, who delivers me through Jesus Christ our Lord!" (Romans 7:24-25A). Call on Jesus sincerely for God's help, and He will be there to save you and deliver you from it, whenever and wherever you call Jesus' precious, powerful and Holy Name, He is with you. See answers to questions 14 and 16.

32. **Do I need to marry a believer, if I plan to get married?**

Since you are the people of our Lord Jesus Christ, "Therefore 'Come out from them and be separate' says the Lord. 'Touch no unclean thing, and I will receive you'. And, 'I will be a Father to you and you will be my sons and daughters, says the Lord Almighty'" (2 Corinthians 6:17-18). "Do not be yoked together with unbelievers. For what do righteousness and wickedness have in common? Or what fellowship can light have with darkness?" (2 Corinthians 6:14). You could be saving yourself from much grief and pain by choosing a fellow believer as a lifelong marriage partner. The marriage relationship can be very challenging enough as it is, without adding an element of different beliefs and values to the mix. There are probably numerous books on how marriage relationships flourish in Christ, so I recommend you speak to your pastor about this subject, and perhaps they can suggest some resources to help shed light on this very important decision. I encourage you to pray for God's help to find a believer to marry for a happy and blessed united life in Christ.

33. **Should I only date believers?**

Yes, as my first response. If you date a believer that you have a lot in common with, it is easier for you to follow God's doctrine. Save yourself time and heartache by praying and asking the Lord to choose a spouse for you.

34. **Can my non-believing fiancé, boyfriend or girlfriend be saved after or through marriage?**

While it is possible that while you are married to an unbeliever you may help to save or convert the unbelieving fiancé, boyfriend, or girlfriend into a believer in Jesus Christ, it is also possible they may not be saved, and this can be extremely trying and difficult for both of you, not to mention any children you may have together. To willfully marry an unbeliever, knowing it is against the wishes of God is asking for trouble and will require a much stronger faith from you in doing so. In general, since it is God's will that you get married to someone who is also a believer in Christ, it is best to do so to have a happy, fruit-filled life. If you came to Christ after marriage and your spouse is not a believer, the Bible instructs us to stay married to be a witness to your spouse. The Bible tells us that our spouse is sanctified through our faith in Jesus. If your unbelieving spouse chooses to leave you, you are not obligated to stay married.

35. **May I divorce after marriage?**

As believers, you are legally and spiritually obligated to honor the covenant of marriage. There are only special circumstances that will allow a Christian couple to divorce after your marriage. If one of the marriage partners commits adultery, or if one person is being physically, mentally, or emotionally abused, divorce is permissible. It is always best to pray fervently and without ceasing for your spouse to change, before choosing divorce. "So, they are no longer two, but one flesh. Therefore, what God has joined together, let no one separate" (Matthew 19:6). "But if you are married to an unbeliever who insists on getting divorced, you may let him/her go. "But if the unbeliever leaves, let it be so. The brother or sister is not bound in such circumstances; God has called us to live in peace" (1 Corinthians 7:15). But if you are a believer, "I tell you that anyone who divorces his wife, except for sexual immorality, and marries another woman commits adultery" (Matthew 19:9). Continue to pray for your spouse and your marriage. God can heal broken hearts and relationships. I encourage you to go to Christian marriage counselling and work on preserving your marriage. Seek the counsel of the pastor at your church, and perhaps they can direct you to Christian marriage counsellors. Your church pastors, your small groups and cell groups can also pray for you and your spouse and marriage.

36. **Can I remain unmarried my whole life as a Christian?**
Paul said "I wish that all of you were as I am. But each of you has your own gift from God; one has this gift, another has that. Now to the unmarried and the widows I say: It is good for them to stay unmarried, as I do. But if they cannot control themselves, they should marry, for it is better to marry than to burn with passion" (1 Corinthians 7:7-9).

But if you have a special calling to be one of Jesus' redeemed holy brides from the Lord to be one of the "144,000" and "...An unmarried woman or virgin is concerned about the Lord's affairs: Her aim is to be devoted to the Lord in both body and spirit," (1 Corinthian 7:34B). That is your special reward from the Lord to you and you can remain unmarried.

In general, as the Lord told us in Genesis "That is why a man leaves his father and mother and is united to his wife, and they become one flesh" (Genesis 2:24). "So, God created mankind in his own image, in the image of God he created them; male and female he created them. God blessed them and said to them, 'Be fruitful and increase in number; fill the earth and subdue it. Rule over the fish of the sea and the birds in the sky and over every living creature that moves on the ground'" (Genesis 1:27-28). From here we can clearly see God's creation of man and woman as "One Flesh" as one marriage between a man and a woman, male and female as one family.

37. **As a young man, may I have sexual relations with my girlfriend before our official marriage?**

No, absolutely not. Sexual activity before an official marriage between a man and a woman is very much prohibited, if you are both believers. "As obedient children, do not conform to the evil desires you had when you lived in ignorance. But just as He who called you is holy, so be holy in all you do; for it is written: "Be holy, because I am Holy" (1 Peter 1:14-15). "Marriage should be honored by all, and the marriage bed kept pure, for God will judge the adulterer and all the sexually immoral" (Hebrews 13:4). Sex is a most wonderful and beautiful gift from the Lord given to a man and a woman to enjoy within the sanctity of their marriage. God gave us the ability to feel amazing sensory pleasure when we physically unite with our spouse. It is through this intimate and special union of love, that the miracle of birth is possible. But this privilege is meant and designed only to be shared between a married couple. If you feel you may have trouble refraining from sex before marriage while dating, discuss this with the person you are dating. Some couples refrain from kissing and holding hands before marriage, so the temptation of sex doesn't overcome them. Depend on the Lord through prayer and in His power in you through the Holy Spirit to fulfill His plans for you and your future spouse. Your marriage will be greatly blessed and enriched when Christ is at the center and when you trust and obey Him in every aspect of your life.

38. **Do I need to have a spiritual partner/mentor?**

As a Christian, it is strongly encouraged to pray for God's will in a good spiritual partner to strengthen you when you are down. Obviously, if your spouse is also a Christian, they can be the best spiritual partner or helper to you. Of course, you can find other spiritual leaders like pastors, district leaders, bishops, elders, and deacons etc. You can always fellowship with him/her to encourage and teach each other in God's words and love in Christ. "Two are better than one, because they have a good return for their labor: If either of them falls down, one can help the other up. But pity anyone who falls and has no one help them up!...Though one may be overpowered, two can defend themselves. A cord of three stands is not quickly broken" (Ecclesiastes 4:9-12). But always remember if there is only two of you, unless you are a married couple, don't communicate or fellowship with each other alone in a private room. It will be better to fellowship in a public area with people around you both.

39.   How do I live a life "set apart for God" in this filthy, corrupted world?

Be Holy, self-controlled, walking in God's Love, praying in the Holy Spirit, examining your heart, and restoring your intimate relationship with the Lord. Ask the Lord to "cleanse" you with His word and Spirit. "But you, dear friends, building yourselves up in your most holy faith and praying in the Holy Spirit, keep yourselves in God's love as you wait for the mercy of our Lord Jesus Christ to bring you to eternal life" (Jude 20-21). Be thankful in everything. "Therefore, with minds that are alert and fully sober, set your hope on the grace to be brought to you when Jesus Christ is revealed at his coming" (1 Peter 1:13). "And now these three remain: faith, hope and love. But the greatest of these is love" (1 Corinthians 13:13). We ought to love our Lord Jesus Christ with all our heart, mind and soul and love our neighbors. The world will tempt you to live as those who don't know Christ's power and love, but you are given power through Jesus Christ to overcome sin and to preach the gospel to everyone the Lord calls you to. You are set apart to live for Jesus and to love others as you love yourself. Trust and rest in the power Jesus gives you to live in this world but not of it.

40. **If I become a Christian, will my life be perfect?**

Eventually, but not in this lifetime. "I have told you these things, so that in me you may have peace. In this world you will have trouble. But take heart! I have overcome the world" (John 16:33). One day we will be with our perfect creator and then your life will be perfect. But until that day, the Lord will give us everything we need to sustain us through all our troubles and storms. Surrender every situation to Jesus and continue to pray for wisdom, grace, strength, and direction. We can trust Jesus to help us no matter what our circumstances are. He will never forsake us or abandon us. He will give us peace that surpasses all understanding, if we surrender the situation, relationship, health issue, fear, decision, plan and every aspect and detail of our lives to Him.

41. **I've given my life to the Lord, why do I sometimes still feel depressed, and not want to get out of bed?**

The enemy is also working to make us feel defeated, lonely, depressed, and unworthy. It is good to pray and ask Jesus to lift the depression. It is also good to read the Bible when you are feeling down. God's word is our comforter, and can heal us. "Whoever dwells in the shelter of the Most High will rest in the shadow of the Almighty. I will say of the Lord He is my refuge and my fortress, my God in whom I trust" (Psalm 91:1-2). If the depression persists, perhaps you should see a doctor about it. God can also choose to heal us through medical attention and medication.

42. **I know I have been forgiven for my sins, but why do I still feel guilty?**

The enemy whispers lies and tries to make us think that God could never forgive us. The enemy tries to separate us from God's love. Satan wants us to think we are not worthy of God's love, forgiveness, or grace. However, when we confess our sins, we are forgiven, and our sins and our guilt are washed away because of Jesus' work on the cross. "For I am convinced that neither death nor life, neither angels or demons, neither the present nor the future, nor any powers, neither height nor depth, nor anything else in all creation, will be able to separate us from the love of

God that is in Christ Jesus our Lord" (Romans 8:38-39). It is important to find a healthy Bible believing church and to get involved in ministry. We are not meant to try to live this life on our own but in conjunction with our 'church family'. We have victory over sin, death, Satan, and guilt through Jesus' work on the cross. Walk in this victory.

43. **I have good friends who are not believers. Do I need to stop associating with them?**

God calls us to be salt and light to the world. He calls us to tell others about Jesus and His work in our lives in hopes that they too would know, believe, and receive God's grace, forgiveness, and salvation. However, if your unbelieving friends are tempting you to take your focus off Jesus and causing you to sin, then it is best to stay away from them and keep praying for them. "Do not conform to the pattern of this world, but be transformed by the renewing of your mind. Then you will be able to test and approve what God's will is– his good, pleasing and perfect will" (Romans 12:2).

44. **I have been lacking money for a long time, is it okay to borrow money from my good Christian friends?**

As a child of God, our God prepared for all in His faithful promises to us: "The Lord is my shepherd, I lack nothing" (Psalm 23:1). If you are suffering due to financial troubles, you should repent and pray first to examine your Christian life and God will answer your prayers and provide what you need. Do not borrow any money from your good Christian friends. If it is God's will for your friend to lend you money, your friend will surely lend you the right amount of funds you need. "Be patient, then, brothers and sisters, until the Lord's coming. See how the farmer waits for the land to yield its valuable crop, patiently waiting for the autumn and spring rains" (James 5:7). Many times, we don't know why God allows us to go through challenges, however, we can trust that God's plans are always the best plans, and we can try and learn from the trials we overcome. We can trust that God uses all things to the good of those who love Him.

45. **May I lend money to a church member?**

First, you should ask for God's will. Is it your personal will or the Lord's will? As a Christian, we should honor and glorify everything from the Lord including our money. If it is the Lord's will, you are encouraged to lend money to your church member to help him/her in need. "Whoever is kind to the poor lends to the LORD, and he will reward them for what they have done" (Proverbs 19:17). However, there are two things you should remember: 1) when you lend money to a friend, no interest is calculated – "Do not take interest or any profit from them, but fear your God, so that they may continue to live among you. You must not lend him money at interest or sell them food at a profit" (Leviticus 25: 36-37), and 2) don't wish for anything in return, rather lend him the money to bless him only – "It is more blessed to give than to receive" (Acts 20:35B).

46. **May I solicit church members for business purposes?**

No, surely not. We should come to church with our minds and hearts set on Him and His purposes, not on how we can make a profit. "Jesus entered the temple area and drove out all who were buying and selling there. He overturned the tables of the money changers and the benches of those selling doves. 'It is written,' He said to them, 'My house will be called a house of prayer,' but you are making it a 'den of robbers'" (Matthew 21: 12-13).

47. **May a church member of the opposite sex be my spiritual partner to fellowship, alone, in a private room?**

No, we suggest you do not fellowship with a church member of the opposite sex in a private room or without any other people or witnesses around. It is better to have good fellowship in God's truth in a public place with other dear brothers and sisters in a group.

48. **May a brother visit or pick up a sister for a church gathering or other purpose by car?**

This is not recommended. It is not good to put yourself in compromising situations. We suggest that if you are a male, that you don't pick up a female by herself. It is good as a male to avoid any unnecessary misunderstanding among the congregation. You might pick up church members of the opposite sex if your brothers and sisters in Christ are with you, or if your spouse is with you.

49. Do I still need to go to work after I've prayed to accept Jesus?

Our Lord Jesus told us our Father, God is working now all the time. Jesus said to them(Jews): "...My Father is always at His work to this very day, and I too, am working" (John 5:17B). Paul also emphasized that we should work diligently in our works. "In the name of the Lord Jesus Christ, we command you, brothers, and sisters, to keep away from every believer who is idle and disruptive and does not live according to teaching you received from us. For you yourselves know how you ought to follow our example. We were not idle when we were with you, nor did we eat anyone's food without paying for it. On the contrary, we worked night and day, laboring and toiling so that we would not be a burden to any of you. We did this, not because we do not have the right to such help, but in order to make ourselves a model for you to imitate. For even when we were with you, we gave you this rule: "The man who is unwilling to work, he shall not eat" (2 Thessalonians 3:6-10).

50. How do I pray and what do I pray about?

"But when you pray, go into your room, close the door and pray to your Father who is unseen. Then your Father, who sees what is done in secret, will reward you, do not keep on babbling like pagans, for they think they will be heard because of their many words. Do not be like them, for your Father knows what you need before you ask him" (Matthew 6:6). "'This, then, is how you should pray: 'Our Father in heaven, hallowed be your name, your kingdom come, your will be done, on earth as it is in heaven. Give us today our daily bread. And forgive us our debts, as we also have forgiven our debtors. And lead us not into temptation, but deliver us from the evil one'" (Matthew 6:9-13).

However, it is important to meditate on Jesus' words and the meaning behind them rather than simply reciting words as a way of trying to earn God's favor. Jesus gave us this example to teach us *how* to pray. He never meant this to be a verbal substitute for intimacy between Himself and us, His creation.

Speak openly and honestly to your Father in Heaven in private. He desires to give you what you ask for according to His perfect and pleasing will.

51. I have no energy even to open my mouth to pray. Is it ok to quit praying?

It is true that our body is sometimes very tired and fatigued, and we want to stop doing everything, including nurturing our relationship with our God through prayer. As our Lord told his disciples:" Watch and pray so that you will not fall into temptation. The spirit is willing, but the flesh is weak" (Matthew 26:41). Give thanks for God's mercy and grace and that He is very understanding about our weakness in praying. He reserves a good helper for us: the Holy Spirit who will pray for you and me. "In the same way, the Spirit helps us in our weakness. We do not know what we ought to pray for, but the Spirit himself intercedes for us through wordless groans. And He who searches our hearts knows the mind of the Spirit, because the Spirit intercedes for the saints in accordance with the will of God" (Romans 8:26-27).

52. Since I believe Jesus sees me and knows me, I have a strong faith in Him. Do I still need to have annual medical check-ups?

You are encouraged to do annual examinations as a good way to honor your body and honor our Lord Jesus.

53. Is it okay for me to grumble or complain about what displeases me?

No, surely not. Never grumble or complain any moment of your life, if you want to be blessed and joyful. God does not like your grumbling, but rather praise and sacrifice with your lips. "Through Jesus, therefore, let us continually offer to God a sacrifice of praise-- the fruit of lips that openly profess his name" (Hebrews 13:15). "And do not grumble, as some of them did—and were killed by the destroying angel" (1 Corinthians 10: 10). You will find spiritual nourishment when you live with an attitude of thankfulness to the Lord. He is the giver of every good and perfect gift. He is exalted when we thank and praise Him in and through all circumstances.

54. **If I read many spiritual books, do I still need to read the Bible?**
Reading the Bible, God's word is like the breath in your lungs as you live your life in Jesus Christ. It may be of some help like "dessert" for you to read spiritual books but not as a "main course" in your daily diet. Jesus said my word is Life and Spirit. There are no other ways to find such nutritious, healthy, and truthful life-giving words as in the Bible, which guide you in your daily walk. "All Scripture is God-breathed and is useful for teaching, rebuking, correcting, and training in righteousness" (2 Timothy 3:16).

55. **What is eternal life? How can I have it?**
Eternal life is life with God forever. Jesus prayed to the Father and said, "Now this is eternal life: that they know you, the only true God, and Jesus Christ, whom you have sent" (John 17:3). It is a new life in Christ you may enjoy today as you live day by day, in His transforming power, with peace and love inside you. "As for you, see that what you have heard from the beginning remains in you. If it does, you also will remain in the Son and in the Father. And this is what He promised us--eternal life" (1 John 2:24-25). If you trust Jesus is God, and you confess your sins, and love and follow Christ, you will have a new spirit and a new heart. You will immediately start living in this splendid eternal life in Jesus' Kingdom forever and forever.

56. **Can my physical body be resurrected?**
Yes, surely your physical body will be resurrected. "For we believe that Jesus died and rose again, and so we believe that God will bring Jesus those who have fallen asleep in him. According to the Lord's word, we tell you that we who are still alive, who are left until the coming of the Lord, will certainly not precede those who have fallen asleep. For the Lord himself will come down from heaven with a loud command with the voice of the archangel and with the trumpet call of God and the dead in Christ will rise first" (1 Thessalonians 4:14-16). "So the other

disciples told him, 'We have seen the Lord!' But he said to them, 'Unless I see the nail marks in his hands and put my finger where the nails were, and put my hand into his side, I will not believe.' A week later his disciples were in the house again, and Thomas was with them. Though the doors were locked, Jesus came and stood among them and said, 'Peace be with you!' Then he said to Thomas, 'Put your finger here; see my hands. Reach out your hand and put it into my side. Stop doubting and believe.' Thomas said to him, 'My Lord and my God!'". (John 20:24-28). So God will raise up our dead body by the power of His Holy Spirit having our spirit matching perfectly with our physical body as a unit becoming a new holy person with Him in His glory. "Dear friends, now we are children of God, and what we will be has not yet been made known. But we know that when Christ appears, we shall be like him, for we shall see him as he is" (1 John 3:2).

57. **Where is my spirit after I die?**

As we all know, a human being has three parts designed perfectly by God: a physical body, a soul, and a spirit. You were born as a perfect combination of a beautifully designed masterpiece created by the Lord. As a Christian, after you die, your spirit will be taken care of. Your spirit will be with Jesus in heaven, your body of flesh will be buried underneath the earth waiting for Jesus to return. Upon Jesus' return, Jesus will take with Him those have "fallen asleep" in Him.

58. **As a Christian, is it all right to kneel and worship family members who have passed away, to show our respect?**

No, as a Christian, the only person we worship or pray to is the Triune God, the Father and Jesus the Son and the Holy Spirit. "I am the LORD your God, who brought you out of Egypt, out of the land of slavery. You shall have no other gods before me" (Exodus 20:2-3).

59. **How will Jesus come and lift me up to heaven while I am alive now on earth?**

Jesus will come together with God the Father in their glory to fulfill His promise to us when He came to earth as a human

142

being. "Do not let your hearts be troubled. You believe in God, believe also in me. My Father's house are many rooms; if that were not so, would I have told you that I am going there to prepare a place for you? And if I go and prepare a place for you, I will come back and take you to be with me that you also may be where I am. You know the way to the place where I am going" (John 14: 1-4).

"After that, we who are still alive and are left will be caught up together with them in the clouds to meet the Lord in the air. And so we will be with the Lord forever. Therefore, encourage each other with these words" (1 Thessalonians 4:17-18).

60. What good thing must I do to get eternal life?

There is nothing you can do nothing to earn your eternal life, it is all from God's grace and mercy given to you through your belief in Him. But as His children we should glorify His name through our lives.

61. There are so many different religions in the world, why do I have to believe in Jesus?

Yes, there exists many different religions, but Only Jesus provides spiritual life. We do not believe in any religion, including Christianity as strictly a religion, but we believe in a true eternal life that can only can be given by Jesus. Despite what some people may claim, all religions do not say the same thing. There are major differences in the truths claimed by each religion. They can all be wrong, but they cannot all be right. Other religions try to provide a way for man to earn his way to God. However, only Jesus provides a way for man to reach God; it is by grace alone, through faith alone.

62. How can I know for sure that Jesus is the only way to God?

No people of other religions can dare to make this declaration as Jesus himself declared:" I am the way and the truth and the life. No one comes to the Father except through me" (John 14:6). "Whoever has the son has life; whoever does not have the Son of God does not have life" (1 John 5:12). "We know also that the Son of God has come and has given us understanding, so that we may know him who is true. And we are in him who is true by being in his Son Jesus Christ. He is the true God and eternal life" (1 John 5:20). What it boils down to is this; Jesus backed up everything he said by raising himself from the dead as witnessed by as many as 500 people at the same time. (1 Corinthians 15:6) The same cannot be said of any other religious figure.

63. **Do I need to share the gospel?**

While we may not be given the opportunity every day, it is the Lord's will that we spread the gospel to those who are perishing (Matthew 28:19-20). This is a great privilege our Lord has given to us, to preach His gospel in this dark world and to pray for more people to have an eternal and glorious life with Him. "He is the one we proclaim, admonishing and teaching everyone with all wisdom, so that we may present everyone fully mature in Christ. To this end I strenuously contend with all the energy Christ so powerfully works in me" (Colossians 1:28-29).

64. **How do I live as a Christian in these end times?**

"The end of all things is near. Therefore, be alert and of sober mind so that you may pray. Above all, love each other deeply, because love covers over a multitude of sins. Offer hospitality to one another without grumbling. Each of you should use whatever gift you have received to serve others as faithful stewards of God's grace in its various forms. If anyone speaks, they should do so as one who speaks the very words of God. If anyone serves, they should do so with the strength God provides, so that in all things God may be praised through Jesus Christ. To him be the power for ever and ever. Amen" (1 Peter 4:7-11). "For the grace of God has appeared that offers salvation to all people. It teaches us to say 'No' to ungodliness and worldly passions, and to live self-controlled, upright and godly lives in this present age, while we wait for the blessed hope—the appearing of the glory of our great God and Savior, Jesus Christ, who gave himself for us to redeem us from all wickedness and to purify for himself a people that are his very own, eager to do what is good" (Titus 2:11-14).

65. **Does a Christian have light in him/her?**

Yes, "In him was life, and that life was the light of all mankind. The light shines in the darkness, and the darkness has not overcome it" (John 1:4-5). If you are still unware of this truth, your spiritual eyes need to be opened by the Holy Spirit to experience it.

66. **How can I get freedom in Christ?**

You need only to understand the truths regarding this, which are in scripture "Now the Lord is the Spirit, and where the Spirit of the Lord is, there is freedom" (2 Corinthians 3:17). "So if the Son sets you free, you will be free indeed" (John 8:36). Amen! Your freedom in Jesus is to worship and serve the Lord. Our belief in Jesus' death on the cross and His resurrection gives us freedom from death, sin, Satan, and guilt.

67. **Now that we are in the end times, what should Christians value and live for most?**

Jesus is coming back. We as Christians should be prepared for His return. Since we don't know when Jesus is returning, we should ensure we are living for Jesus. Our lives should be a living sacrifice. We can worship the Lord with our lives by loving, following, obeying, and trusting Jesus. Trusting and loving Jesus gives us "eternal life" with God. "Eternal Life with God" is our biggest and most precious hope and gift. We should also share God's love with our neighbors. Jesus calls us to be witnesses to the ends of the earth, making disciples of all people and baptizing them in the name of the Father, and of the Son and of the Holy Spirit.

68. **Do you have a brand new and resurrected life in you? Are you living for Jesus?**

Yes or No? If you wish to discuss this further, you may contact me for more information. May God bless you with a wonderful and miraculous life!

CONCLUSION

I encourage every Christian believer to become what God created them to be: a child of God, living a life that testifies that Jesus is alive. If His life is in you, shining upon you, the power of the Holy Spirit has surely resurrected you already.

We are not Christians who just sit in church "listening to more sermons" without "carrying our own crosses, denying ourselves and following Jesus". God is love, love is to know God, to love God and to love our neighbors. Love is Jesus' sacrifice for us on the cross and He is God's love and our Lord and Savior. "And this is his command: to believe in the name of His Son, Jesus Christ, and to love one another as He commanded us. The one who keeps God's commands lives in him, and he in them. And this is how we know that he lives in us: We know it by the Spirit He gave us" (1 John 3:23-24). What is love? "Love is patient, love is kind. It does not envy, it does not boast, it is not proud. It does not dishonor others, it is not self-seeking, it is not easily angered, it keeps no record of wrongs. Love does not delight in evil but rejoices with the truth. It always protects, always trusts, always hopes, always perseveres. Love never fails" (1 Corinthians 13:4-8A). "If I have the gift of prophecy and can fathom all mysteries and all knowledge, and if I have a faith that can move mountains, but have not love, I am nothing. If I give all I possess to the poor and give over my body to hardship that I may boast, but do not have love, I gain nothing" (1 Corinthians 13:2-3). What a gracious warning to each of us for this walk in Christ. "No love, No Life – Life is in Christ!"

Let's start with the most basic of God's commands today, to live a life of Jesus Christ, by showing Him our fruit. "But the fruit of the Spirit is love, joy, peace, forbearance, kindness, goodness, faithfulness, gentleness and self-control… Since we live by the Spirit, let us keep in step with the Spirit. Let us not become conceited, provoking and envying each other" (Galatians 5:22-26).

We have nothing good in this world apart from Jesus. We are nothing, have nothing to be proud about, and have nothing to boast about. We are just like dust, apart from Jesus we have NO life.

"The life of mortals is like grass, they flourish like a flower of the field; the wind blows over it and it is gone, and its place remembers it no more" (Psalm 103:15-16). Again, Moses also wrote: "You turn people back to dust, saying, 'Return to dust, you mortals'. A thousand years in your sight are like a day that has just gone by, or like a watch in the night. Yet you sweep people away in the sleep of death--they are like the new grass of the morning: In the morning it springs up new, but by evening it is dry and withered. We are consumed by your anger and terrified by your indignation. You have set our iniquities before you, our secret sins in the light of your presence. All our days pass away under your wrath; we finish our years with a moan. Our days may come to seventy years or eighty, if our strength endures; yet the best of them are but trouble and sorrow, for they quickly pass, and we fly away" (Psalm 90:3-10).

God loves us. We can't use Jesus for our own purposes for our own fleshly pleasures. As Paul emphasized in the book of Philippians 3:19 regarding such people, "Their destiny is destruction, their god is their stomach, and their glory is in their shame. Their mind is on earthly things." Believers shouldn't doubt. We need to be rooted in God's Word daily to grow in our faith. We learn from Jesus' teaching of the disciples. As we learn more about who God is, we discipline ourselves to be more self-controlled in God's truth, love, and Spirit.

The Holy Spirit empowers us and helps us to overcome our sins. The Holy Spirit is the best helper and counselor. "But you will receive power when the Holy Spirit comes on you; and you will be my witnesses in Jerusalem, and in all Judea and Samaria, and to the ends of the earth" (Acts 1:8). "But very truly I tell you, it is for your good that I am going away. Unless I go away, the Advocate will not come to you; but if I go, I will send him to you" (John 16:7). "Therefore, there is now no condemnation for those who are in Christ Jesus, because through Christ Jesus the law of the Spirit who gives life has set you free from the law of sin and death. For what the law was powerless to do because it was weakened by the flesh, God did by sending his own Son in the likeness of sinful flesh to be a sin offering" (Romans 8:1-3).

The Holy Spirit guides, teaches, corrects, convicts us of sin and even shows what is yet to come. He helps us to choose Jesus and obey His teachings and commands to love Him the way that Jesus instructed. Sometimes when we don't obey God, we will surely suffer in vain. The closer we get to Jesus, the more He matures our character and our faith. God's will is revealed to us as we draw closer to Jesus and obey His voice. However, Christians are not immune to sin or difficult times. In our walk with our Lord, we may also encounter trials and challenges, more than we enjoy a stress-free life. In the midst of these hardships, suffering and pain, believers are drawn closer to Christ. "Followers of Jesus are destined to be transformed into Jesus' likeness - the very 'Image of Christ', and it is certain that the journey of this "conforming' involves suffering and pain.

Many Christians don't have the will to endure the suffering and the trials life brings. They may fall away from their faith and lose hope in Jesus, or become angry with God. We need to ask God's face to shine upon us for repentance, daily asking for His blood and glory to clean and sanctify us. We as Christian believers must be humble and suffer for God's kingdom, to receive His blessings. We should be joyful in our suffering in Christ for Jesus' Kingdom as Paul said: "Not only so, but we also glory in our sufferings, because we know that suffering produces perseverance; perseverance, character; and character, hope. And hope does not put us to shame, because God's love has been poured out into our hearts through the Holy Spirit, who has been given to us" (Romans 5:3-5). "So we fix our eyes not on what is seen, but on what is unseen, since what is seen is temporary, but what is unseen is eternal" (2 Corinthians 4:18). "But the one who stands firm to the end will be saved. And this gospel of the kingdom will be preached in the whole world as a testimony to all nations, and then the end will come" (Matthew 24:13-14).

I am so firm in this belief as Paul said, "If indeed we share in his sufferings in order that we may also share in his glory" (Romans 8:17B). We have such confidence and faith in our Lord Christ before God. "Not that we are competent in ourselves to claim anything for ourselves, but our competence comes from God" (2 Corinthians 3:5).

I can't do anything of eternal value without God's Spirit in my heart and without His vision: "Where there is no revelation, people cast off restraint; but blessed is the one who heeds wisdom's instruction" (Proverbs 29:18). The Holy Spirit helps us understand His perfect will for us and for our future. Sometimes our faith is so extreme. It is at these times, we need to ask ourselves, is this God's will or my own desire and strength? "This is the confidence we have in approaching God: that if we ask anything according to his will, he hears us-- whatever we ask--we know that we have what we asked of him" (1 John 5:14-15).

As Apostle Paul instructed us: "Rejoice in the Lord always. I will say it again; Rejoice! Let your gentleness be evident to all. The Lord is near. Do not be anxious about anything, but in every situation, by prayer and petition, with thanksgiving, present your requests to God. And the peace of God, which transcends all understanding, will guard your hearts and your minds in Christ Jesus." (Philippians 4: 4-7). The new life in Christ is a Resurrected Life in you my dear brothers and sisters: this is eternal life in you, for you have been chosen to serve our Lord Jesus as His instrument. Our Lord resurrected me thirty-five years ago with His Holy power and gave me a new resurrected life, so He can raise your spiritually dead life to a new resurrected life in Christ as well. Just as one song by Elevation Worship proclaims:

"By your spirit, I will rise from the ashes of defeat,
The resurrected King is resurrecting me,
In Your name,
I come alive to declare Your victory,
The resurrected King is resurrecting me."

"He Must Become Greater; I Must Become Less" (John 3:30). This should be our motto in the attitude of our hearts as we serve the Lord. "May the grace of the Lord Jesus Christ, and the love of God, and the fellowship of the Holy Spirit be with you all" (2 Corinthians 13:14). This can be our daily encouragement. May God our Lord Jesus Christ bless you, keep you and protect you with His richest love, surrounding you all the time from now to the end of time.

As my prayer to encourage each of us, I am ending with "It is written: 'I believed; therefore, I have spoken.' Since we have that same spirit of faith, we also believe and therefore speak, because we know that the one who raised the Lord Jesus from the dead will also raise us with Jesus and present us with you to himself. All this is for your benefit, so that the grace that is reaching more and more people may cause thanksgiving to overflow to the glory of God" (2 Corinthians 4:13-15).

Finally, as my sincere thanks and appreciation and as a challenge to you, I encourage you to take my witness story as a gospel flyer to share and circulate among your friends, relatives, neighbors, believers, or unbelievers to demonstrate your love for others, as we love and serve our wonderful Lord Jesus.

He who has an ear, let him hear what the Spirit says to YOU!

You are chosen to be loved and to show love; to share His gospel as a special Envoy and Ambassador of the Lord Jesus Christ.

I have been resurrected for this glorious life now, have you?

About Author
PETER PAN SHI

The First Intern from P.R. China at United We Stand
and Senior Research Fellow of the World Association
of the Former United We Stand Interns and Fellows:
An Official United We Stand Peace Messenger;

Honorable International Goodwill Ambassador;

Disciple, Evangelist, Deacon, and Preacher of the
gospel form Christian Zion Church Los Angeles;

From Dead to Alive; From a poor boy in a remote village to
an International Evangelist at the UWS Communities;

From a rebelling and prideful unbeliever to an
obedient and humble servant of the Lord;

From physically and spiritually dead to miraculously
and abundantly alive in Christ;

A man of miracles upon miracles and grace upon
grace being granted by the Lord to be a Witness and
Special Ambassador for Christ Jesus; and

A man whose name was prophesized by the Lord as "Peter" Pan
Shi – "Fisher of Men" who has commissioned his resurrected life
to the Spreading of the gospel of Jesus Christ in the world.

Printed in the United States
By Bookmasters